SET THE CAPTIVES FREE

FREEDOM. ARE YOU WILLING TO PAY THE PRICE?

Tom Snow

JUST TO BE CLEAR TEACHING SERIES

Light, Truth, Blood

Get 3 Exclusive Free Resources

Thank you for purchasing SET THE CAPTIVES FREE.

As a thank you, SCAN here to get your 3 Exclusive Resources available to you, today.

When there you'll have the option to sign up for our occasional Substack Posts and get the Free Exclusive Resources—Not available to anyone elsewhere.

Don't worry, you can cancel anytime and still keep your Resources.

—Tom Snow

DEDICATION

I DEDICATE THIS BOOK to the Lord Jesus Christ, the Holy Spirit, and Papa God, the Father.

I also dedicate it to my wonderful wife, Danielle, and my daughter Juliette, who likewise love the Lord.

CONTENTS

NOTES

SOURCES

V ERSES OR VERSE FRAGMENTS originate from the New American Standard Version Bible (NASB)®, New International Version Bible (NIV)®, The Amplified Bible (AMP)®, The King James Version Bible (KJV)®, or Strong's® Greek and Hebrew original texts; citations may or may not be included. All other names, trademarks, and any other such rights are owned by their respective originators. All other rights are reserved.

FOREWORD

As Jesus said in Luke 4:18,

"**T**HE SPIRIT OF THE Lord is on me, because He has *Anointed* me to proclaim *Good News* to the poor. He has sent me to *Proclaim Freedom* for the prisoners and *Recovery* of *Sight* for the *Blind*, to *SET* the *OPPRESSED [CAPTIVES] FREE.*"

Jesus was quoting from Isaiah 61:1,

"The Spirit of the Lord God is upon Me, because the Lord has *Anointed* and *Qualified* Me to proclaim *Good News* to the poor [to preach the Gospel of good tidings to the meek, the poor, and afflicted]; He has sent me to *BIND UP* and *HEAL* the *BROKENHEARTED*, to *PROCLAIM LIBERTY [FREEDOM]* to the [*PHYSICAL* and *SPIRITUAL*] *CAPTIVES* and the *OPENING* of the *PRISON* and of the *EYES* to *THOSE WHO ARE BOUND* [and *RELEASE* from *DARKNESS* for the *PRISONERS*]."

INTRODUCTION

THE FIRST BOOK, ***THE DAILY STAND,*** contained many humorous and fun true stories of God's miraculous power. This book will not center on such. While this book incorporates numerous true stories, it will address very serious topics needing immediate attention in the Church.

In this book we will discuss many very extremely important subjects. Future books already planned for this series will feature many more fun true stories of God's Power for you to read. So, stay tuned and follow along.

Nevertheless, for now, please continue reading this material so ***ALL*** the ***Captives*** can be ***Set Free!***

QUOTES FROM READERS

This book will challenge everything you believe about church and freedom.

This book will cause controversy. Those being set free will love it. Those wanting to maintain captivity will hate it.

This is a once in a lifetime work, directly from the heart of the Father, to release His children from all the things that hold them captive and keep them from walking free in Him.

It's a must-read for ALL believers.

You better be ready to have your faith tested.

This book contains the refiner's fire.

After reading this book, ALL leaders (at every level) will want (need) to reevaluate their positions and responsibilities over God's flock; as well as what God will require of them, holding them into account.

It's a real gut wrencher.

Be ready to be tested if you have a religious spirit.

This book will test you in many ways.

You may not be as safe as you thought.

If you're convinced you're safe, you're probably not.

If you're ready to argue that you're not the ones being talked about here, you're probably wrong.

If you think your theology or your religion will save you, it won't.

Buckle up, you're in for a challenging ride.

Will you put down this book and throw away this opportunity just so you can bury your head in the sand to pretend you're "ok"?

Are you willing to take the test?

Do you want to remain bound/captive? If not, then read this book like your life depends upon it, so you can learn how to throw off the chains and join those being set free.

CHAPTER ONE

WHAT YOU MIGHT THINK THIS BOOK IS ABOUT

BUT MOST LIKELY YOU'D BE WRONG

YOU MIGHT THINK THIS book will focus on deliverance—since many authors have written many books on this subject—to set captives free. Yet, while an important area, this book is not about that subject.

Many people, including God's people, need deliverance to be set free from many kinds of (evil) spirits that oppress or possess them, as discussed in the first book, *THE DAILY STAND*—but that's not the topic to be covered here.

You might think this book will emphasize people being held captive under sin. Yet, again, while an important area, this book will not center on that subject.

Many people, including God's people, do need to be set free from sin(s) that rule their lives, as discussed in the first book—but that's not the main focus of this book.

You might think this book is about people held captive in physical, mental, or emotional afflictions. Yet, again, while an important area, this book is not about that subject.

Many people, including God's people, do need to be set free from these afflictions that can plague their lives in many ways—but that's not the topic to be covered here.

You might think this book is about innocent children or other people that are being held in bondage as slaves (for work) or sex slaves. Yet, again, while an absolutely heart-breaking and vitally important area, this book is not about that subject.

Many innocent children or other people need to be set free from such unimaginable enslavement—but that's not the topic to be covered here.

Instead, this book is about many of God's people, the Body of Christ, the Church, the Saints being held captive in many areas and in many ways. I will discuss these things in the upcoming chapters.

I will discuss some mind-blowing things—depending upon your experience with God. As well as, I will elaborate on some recent events that were the impetus to writing this book.

For my next book, I had planned to write **BREAKING THE CURSE OF THE GENERATIONS**, following my first book, but the Lord preempted that plan. He redirected me, my heart broken, as I prayed for two wonderful but severely "captured" sisters. We'll talk more about them and others in a later chapter.

Believers being taken Captive

Please note: throughout this book, I will talk a great deal or refer to things presented in depth from the first book [and manual], ***THE DAILY STAND***. When I mention or refer to things from the first book, I may not spend the time to go into depth on those subjects, here, nor repeat all the scriptures or Greek and Hebrew. So, for anyone who hasn't read the first book, please take the time to pause here and go read it so that you will understand how *ALL* these things connect.

CHAPTER TWO

AREAS OF CAPTIVITY

THE "LARGEST AREA OF CAPTIVITY IS BETWEEN THE EARS"

LET'S TALK ABOUT THE MIND

INSIDE OUR MINDS, HOLD all our thoughts, and within our hearts, all our beliefs—good, bad, or ugly. Here, we fight the battle between good and evil, deciding which to listen to.

From the beginning, the devil, the *god* of this world, has trained us to run his maze. Yes, we are nothing more than mice to him. Ring one bell one way and we'll respond as trained. Ring another bell another way and we'll respond to the next. Click a buzzer in our thoughts and we respond again. Send electrical shocks in different degrees and we'll act according to all our programming.

This is a given.

We cannot change it.

It's the stronghold the *god* of this world has absolutely programmed in us and has absolute control over—no ifs, ands, or buts. The bible calls it our "old nature," the "old self," the "old man," or the "flesh."

We talked about this subject in the first book. Let's review a few things again and then elaborate more.

In Ephesians 4:17-24 it says,

"So this I say, and affirm together with the Lord, that you walk no longer just as the Gentiles also walk, in the futility of their mind,

Being darkened in their understanding, excluded from the life of God because of the ignorance that is in them, because of the hardness of their heart;

And they, having become callous, have given themselves over to sensuality for the practice of every kind of impurity with greediness.

But you did not learn **Christ** in this way,

If indeed you have heard Him and have been taught in Him, just as truth is in Jesus,

That, in reference to your former manner of life, you lay aside the *old self*, which is being corrupted in accordance with the lusts of deceit,

And that you be *renewed* in the *spirit* of *your mind*,

And put on the *new self*, which in the likeness of God has been created in righteousness and holiness of the truth."

Do you remember what you learned in the first book about **Christ**? That Christ is not Jesus's last name. In the Greek, it means the *Anointing* by the Holy Spirit. That it's **Christ [the Anointing]** in you that's the **Hope** of **Glory**. That we were sealed with the **Holy Spirit [the Anointing]** of promise on the day of our salvation until the day of redemption, as told in

Ephesians 1:13-14,

"In Him, you also, after listening to the message of truth, the gospel of your salvation—having also believed, you were **Sealed** in **Him** with the **Holy Spirit** of **Promise**, who is given as a **Pledge** of our inheritance, with a view to the redemption of God's own possession, to the praise of His glory."

Therefore, since we've been sealed with the Holy Spirit [by a pledge] until the day of redemption and since the Holy Spirit is God, who is **Perfect**, now lives within us, wouldn't that mean that we have forever put away, finished with, removed, destroyed, and eliminated the old man? Shouldn't it be *"GONE," "OVER," "PAST," "DONE WITH"* forever? Since God is **Perfect**, wasn't this process *"ONCE and DONE?"*

Unfortunately, No.

IT'S A PLEDGE OF WHAT'S TO COME—NOT A GUARANTEE

In Second Corinthians 1:21-22 we're told about the pledge again,

"Now He who establishes us with you in *Christ* and *Anointed* us is God, who also sealed us and gave us the Spirit in our hearts as a **Pledge**."

In Romans 6:1-19 we're told,

"What shall we say then? Are we to continue in sin so that grace may increase?

May it never be! How shall we who died to sin still live in it?

Or do you not know that all of us who have been **baptized** into **Christ** *[the **Anointing**]* Jesus have been baptized into His death?

Therefore, we have been buried with Him through baptism into death, so that as **Christ** *[the **Anointing**]* was **raised** from the **dead** through the glory of the Father, so we too might **walk** in **newness** of *life*.

For if we have become united with Him in the likeness of His death, certainly we shall also be in the likeness of His resurrection,

Knowing this, that our **old self** was **crucified** with **Him**, in order that our body of sin might be done away with, so that we would no longer be slaves to sin; for he who has died is freed from sin.

Now if we have died with **Christ** *[the **Anointing**]*, we believe that we shall also live with Him, knowing that **Christ** *[the **Anointing**]*, having been raised from the dead, is never to die again; death no longer is master over Him.

For the death that He died, He died to sin once for all; but the life that He lives, He lives to God.

Even so, consider yourselves to be dead to sin, but alive to God in **Christk** *[the **Anointing**]* Jesus.

Therefore, do not let sin reign in your mortal body so that you obey its lusts...

For sin shall not be master over you, for you are not under law but under grace.

What then? Shall we sin because we are not under law but under grace? *May it never be!*

Do you not know that when you **present yourselves** to someone as **slaves** for **Obedience**, you are **slaves** of the one whom you **obey**, either of sin resulting in death, or of obedience resulting in righteousness?

But thanks be to God that though you were slaves of sin, you became obedient from the heart to that form of teaching to which you were committed,

And having been freed from sin, you became **Slaves** of **Righteousness**.

I am speaking in human terms because of the weakness of your flesh. For just as you *presented* your members as slaves to impurity and to lawlessness, resulting in further lawlessness, so now **Present** your **members** as **Slaves** to **Righteousness**, *resulting in* **SANCTIFICATION**."

THERE'S THE KEY—SANCTIFICATION!

Sanctification is a process in each and every one of us that takes a **Lifetime** to complete.

Yes, the promised Holy Spirit saved and sealed us on the day we invited the Lord into our lives, but that's when the **REAL WORK** began.

In Acts 26:18, as Paul is explaining to King Agrippa why he was chosen to go to the Gentiles, he said,

"To open their eyes so that they may turn from darkness to light and from the dominion of Satan to God, that they may receive forgiveness of sins and an inheritance among those *who have been* **Sanctified** by faith in Jesus."

Here *who have been* **Sanctified** is the Greek word 'hagiazō' (hah-gē-a-zō), which means, *"to **make holy**," "consecrate," "sanctify," "hallowed," "keep himself holy," "sanctified," "sanctifies"*—which comes from the root word 'hagios' (hah-gē-os) meaning *"**sacred**," "holy," "**Holy of Holies**," "holy one," "**holy place**," "most holy," "**saint**," "**saints**," "sanctuary."*

Let's take a quick tangent to realize that the **Lifelong Process** of **Sanctification**, making us and keeping us holy, is a *GIFT* from God to allow us to enter the 'hagios' (hah-gē-os), the *"**Holy of Holies**."* Do you remember the Tabernacle God gave the Israelites in the wilderness? It had three distinctive areas: the Outer Court, the Holy Place, and the **Holy of Holies**, where God lived. Everyone who wanted to find God could come into the Outer Court to cleanse themselves and give burnt offerings. Then, and only then, could they proceed into the Holy Place. But in the Old Testament times, only the High Priest (singular) could enter the **Holy of Holies**—and that was iffy sometimes. It wasn't until Jesus died and the curtain was ripped in two that Believers, Saints, had a path to come into the Holy of Holies where God lives.

Did you note that the word 'hagiazō' (hah-gē-a-zō) not only defines the process of *Sanctification* as the only way of access into the **Holy of Holies**, but also defines what are true **Saints?** Meaning that this same **Lifelong Process** of **Sanctification,** by the Holy Spirit working in us, causes us to become **Saints.** Therefore, becoming a **Saint** [in the true biblical sense, not in religious "sainthood" *false Beliefs*] is *NOT* a given—which we, as Christian Believers, unfortunately have just taken for granted—by our lack of knowledge.

Moving on, this same Greek word 'hagiazō' (hah-gē-a-zō) is used as **Sanctified** in Second Timothy 2:20-21,

"But in a great house there are not only vessels of gold and silver, but also [utensils] of wood and earthenware, and some for honorable and noble [use] and some for menial and ignoble [use].

So whoever cleanses himself [from what is ignoble and unclean, who separates himself from contact with contaminating and corrupting influences] will [then himself] be a vessel set apart and useful for honorable and noble purposes, **Sanctified,** consecrated and profitable to the Master, fit and ready for any good work."

Another word for **Sanctification** in the Greek is 'hagiasmos' (hah-gē-as-MOS) which is from 'hagiazō' (hah-gē-a-zō), and means, *"consecration,"* **"sanctification,"** **"sanctifying work,"** *"sanctity,"* and denotes a current, ongoing, and lifelong process.

In Second Thessalonians 2:13-14 we're told,

"But we, brethren beloved by the Lord, ought and are obligated [as those who are in debt] to give thanks always to God for you, because God chose you from the beginning as His first fruits (first converts) for salvation through the **Sanctifying Work** of the [Holy] Spirit and [your] belief in (adherence to, trust in, and reliance on) the Truth.

[It was] to this end that He called you through our Gospel, so that you may obtain and share in the glory of our Lord Jesus **Christ (*the* Anointing).*"*

Let's reread Romans 6:19 in the AMP:

"I am speaking in familiar human terms because of your natural limitations. For as you [*presented*] **Yielded** your bodily members [and faculties] as servants to impurity and ever-increasing lawlessness, so now [*present*] **Yield** your bodily members [and faculties] once for all as servants to righteousness (right being and doing) [which leads] to **Sanctification.***"*

Seeing that "presenting" is "yielding" and remembering everything the first book taught you about **Yielding;** we recognize that **Yielding** is an ongoing, lifelong, daily, moment-by-moment process which *leads to* **Sanctification.** And that process will remain incomplete for as long as we live on Earth.

Again in Romans 6:22,

"But now, having been freed from sin and enslaved to God, you derive your benefit, **Resulting *in* Sanctification,** and the outcome, eternal life."

Note the wording, *"**Resulting in.***"* I love that this defines the end result of the lifelong process, which has predetermined results for our benefit (for our good)!

Again in First Peter 1:1-2,

"To those...who are chosen according to the foreknowledge of God the Father, by the **Sanctifying Work** of the Spirit, to obey Jesus Christ and be sprinkled with His blood: May grace and peace be yours in the fullest measure."

Once again, let me repeat, it's the **Sanctifying Work** of the Spirit of God in us—it's not a given—it's a process that only we can allow by **Choice** and **Yielding.**

THE SECRET IS TO REMAIN IN CHRIST

In Second Corinthians 5:17,

"Therefore, if anyone is *in **Christ** [in the **Anointing**]*, he is a new creature; the old things passed away; behold, new things have come."

Just to repeat from earlier, we talked a great deal in the first book about what **IN Christ** means and how to live in and operate out of that place, so I will not repeat it here. If you haven't read the first book, **THE DAILY STAND**, please pause and read it to understand how *ALL* these things, in this book and the rest, interconnect.

FOUR VOICES

WHO ARE WE LISTENING TO?

One, the voice we are hearing might be from God, He with the big "G". The True and Living God of Israel who created the Heavens, the Earth, and the Universe—who still (constantly) holds all of it (everything) together by the Word of His Mouth.

Two, the voice we are hearing might be from the *god* of this world (or his cohorts), he with the little "g" talking from the outside—or worse, we may hear from demons occupying our inner spaces.

Three, the voice we are hearing might be from us and our old self that was taught everything we know, from the beginning, by the *god* of this world.

By the way, in case you haven't realized it yet, number two and three will sound the same to us—hardly distinguishable to most, if not all—because we were so well-trained.

Or, four, the voice we are hearing might be from [many] others who we've allowed (given permission) to have influence over us—unknowingly or not.

I WILL LEAVE HEARING FROM GOD FOR LAST

Many believers think they know the voice of God and won't make the same mistakes that others might make—but for that reason alone, they will make those mistakes over and over—then someday wonder why.

Like the 'ol devil on one shoulder and the angel on the other—continually whispering into our ears—we hear a constant bombardment of voices. Thoughts of every kind. Some learn to tune it out—which might be beneficial in one way—blocking the voices of the enemy and our maze-trained internal voices. But if we desire to hear from the Lord, He with the big "L", then tuning out everything becomes self-defeating.

So learning how to distinguish the voice of God from others becomes vital to our spiritual health.

THE POWER OF THE AIR

In the first book, we discussed in great detail about the Power of the Air. How the enemy uses many forms of influence to speak into our lives—the most devious being, the whispering in our ears as the polar opposite of hearing God's still small voice.

The devil has been ruling over us since the beginning. He's taught us to run the maze. As the ruler of the world, he controlled all our thoughts, beliefs, feelings, and influence.

That is until we gave our lives to the Lord. Then he lost influence over us. But guaranteed he didn't give up the fight. He constantly attempts to lure us back to the influences (voices) of our upbringing and regain his control.

Therefore, as well-trained mice, we can become our own worst enemy. Even if we learn how to walk in God's Authority (as taught in the first book) and cut off the enemy's presence and influence, we are well-trained and, without intervention, will do the enemy's job for him.

HEARING FROM THE INSIDE

We discussed oppression and possession in great detail in the first book. When fallen angels, demons, spirits oppress or possess areas in or around us, these beings overwhelm us with thoughts and feelings, compelling us to remain captive. For whatever reason we allowed, or worse, agreed, that these spirits could take up residence [forever]. They will compel us to do their bidding until released from their captivity.

You will learn more about this in the upcoming chapter, "TYPES OF CAPTIVITY."

WE CAN BE OUR OWN WORST ENEMY

We are so well-trained that the devil can sit back and laugh as we (most likely) will fall back to our deeply embedded training. The devil and his cohorts don't need to do much of anything—just "ring the bell" and we'll gladly take over (by our old nature) and become the ones dictating to ourselves what we are to do. Then, if we ever question those voices, we will end up arguing against ourselves. That catch-22 is a no-win situation and the devil's delight.

VOICES OF OTHERS

Who have we allowed to have influence over us?

Was it our parents?

Was it school teachers as we grew up?

Was it pastors, leaders, or others in churches?

Was it mentors from other sources, areas, or times in our lives?

Were they (hopefully) "for good" or were they "inherently" or "hiddenly" evil?

Most likely, some of each.

These influential voices of others from our lives resound in our ears and throughout our beings. While some voices serve good, many originate from their father, the ruler of this world, who taught them.

How can we know the difference? Stay tuned and learn.

WHAT ARE SOME THINGS THESE VOICES SAY TO US?

Let's look at some examples, starting with self-image views:

How about when we say or think, "I don't have a good image [view] of myself [or who I am]"? Comparing this or that area in our lives—areas we view as lacking—when comparing ourselves to others. Not liking this or that about ourselves. Maybe even causing eating or mental disorders for some because of it—in some fashion or another. This is a negative view from the outside in.

Then we have, "You don't believe you have self-worth." This differs from self-image. This is a negative view from the inside out. Self-worth is evaluating if we have value to anyone, including ourselves. Do you have negative self-talk beliefs going on inside? Maybe raging inside? Sometimes? All the time? Do you drown yourself in self-contempt?

How about, "You don't have a good body-image (view) of yourself." Too big? Too small? Too short? Too tall? Too heavy? Too skinny? I don't like my hair—length, color, type, etc.? I don't like my skin color? Believing others view you the same (negative) ways you do.

You may not have a good view of what you think of yourself in one or many areas. Like: "I'm a loser" or "I mess up everything." Can you name others about yourself?

You may not have a good view of what others think of you. Like: "They know I have all these problems," and "I'm sure that their 'less than perfect look'," or "Their 'less than perfect response'," proves it.

Do you think, say or feel this way about any of these things?

"Death and life are in the power of the tongue—with every word we are creating or tearing down." [Quoted from Dallas Malloy, *"Stand Up and Fight: Words of Courage from a Women's Boxing Pioneer to Unlock Your Faith and Conquer Fear",* Lord & J.J. Press.]

It's important to note all these negative thoughts, including anxiety, worry, and doubt, if left unchecked, turn into the words we say and become tools for the enemy to tear us down.

Are you afraid to let God's light into every room of your mind, heart, soul, feelings, and being?

Does the thought of the darkness that could be uncovered scare you?

You might "fight" against these thoughts, but know that they are a genuine struggle that many face regularly.

Did you notice that all these things happen between the ears?

HOW ABOUT BELIEFS?

Do you believe in good or evil? How do you define them? Are they black and white—the devil versus God—or do you believe in many shades of gray?

Do you believe you deserve good things, or do you believe you deserve bad things in life? Or maybe some of each?

Do you think other people believe you deserve good or bad things in life?

What do we believe we must do to gain acceptance?

What have we been taught?

Have others' *Belief Systems* had a major influence over our lives?

HOW ABOUT THE HEART?

Are your emotions good or bad?

Are your feelings good or bad?

What things do you hold on to at a deeper level, versus just the thoughts that pass through your mind?

WHAT ABOUT OTHER AREAS?

Do you wrestle with unforgiveness? Do you forgive *EVERYONE* all the time for everything?

What about judgements? Do you wrestle with them? Are you judgement free?

How are you with course jesting? The kind that actually belittles, degrades, harshly pokes fun, or demeans others.

How about OCD?

How about being a germaphobe?

Do fears, phobias control you or any part of your thinking or life?

Do you wrestle with these or other mental conditions?

Do you need to take medications for such mental challenges?

Are you a workout freak?

Are you a workaholic?

Or to the other side, someone who avoids such?

Are you lazy?

Do you overeat? If so, do you know why?

Do you have a problem with alcohol or drugs? If so, do you know why you do?

Do you have a problem with sins that *plague* your life? Not just the act of simple mistakes that we *ALL* make. But things when we get "taken away" or "caught up in" them, they can capture us; such as,

Lusting after "things" versus normal functions or desires?

The misuse of sex?

The misuse of food?

The love of money?

Wanting power and control?

WHY SO MANY QUESTIONS?

Because these denote just a few of the many areas that can consume us. Some a little. Some a lot. Some overwhelmingly. Noting that these many, sometimes overwhelming, thought processes or areas can come from many sources.

HOW ABOUT YOUR RELATIONSHIP WITH GOD?

[HE WITH THE BIG "G"]

Do you believe in Him?

Do you have a personal relationship with the Lord?

Do you try to walk with God? And allow Him to walk with you?

Do you try to talk to and hear from God?

FURTHER: IN ADDITION ABOUT HEARING FROM GOD

Do you think you hear from Him regularly?

Or not so much?

Maybe a little?

Maybe a lot?

Maybe often?

Maybe daily?

Some days more than others?

Maybe all the time?

The first book explains many things about learning to walk with the True and Living God, the God of Israel, the God who created all things in the Heavens, the Earth, and the Universe. Who still holds all of those things together by the word of His mouth.

If you're a person who has walked with God, been genuinely humbled by the Spirit of God, not someone pretending in fake spirituality or fake religiosity, you would answer that,

"For *[NOW]* our knowledge is fragmentary (incomplete and imperfect), and our prophecy (our teaching) is fragmentary (incomplete and imperfect).

But when the complete and (total) perfect comes, the incomplete and imperfect will vanish away (become antiquated, void, and superseded).

When I was a child, I talked like a child, I thought like a child, I reasoned like a child; *NOW* that I have become a man, I am done with childish ways and have put them aside.

[Yet] for *NOW* we are looking in a mirror that gives only a dim (blurred) reflection [of reality as in a riddle or enigma], but then [when perfection comes—when we stand before Him] we shall see in reality and face to face! *NOW* I know in part (imperfectly), but then I shall know and understand fully and clearly, even in the same manner as I have been fully and clearly known and understood [by God]." (1 Corinthians 13:9-12 AMP)

If you'd answered otherwise—such that you hear perfectly, 100 percent of the time or even close—or think [or believe] your walk is just as Perfect, you're *full of CRAP*, and in need of the Truth!

Instead, let us adopt a proper position to walk humbly before our God.

CHAPTER THREE

BELIEF SYSTEMS ~ THE STOCKHOLM SYNDROME

THE ENTICEMENT

LIKE TREASURE HUNTERS ENTHRALLED by the dream of achieving the impossible, to have that treasure for themselves and then show off to the world [who just thought that they were "dreamers", "wasting their lives away"] that they **DID IT**—that they **DO** have *Self-Worth* and *Deserve Respect!*

In the same way, temptations, lures, and incentives dupe many into volunteering for captivity.

Whether it's for:

Something which fosters self-respect and/or respect from others.

Something that boosts their self-esteem.

Something that improves their health in various ways.

Something that gives them wealth [in many areas or ways]. This may include actual dollars, but it's not limited to money.

Something bestowing GIFTS upon them in various ways.

Giving them something strong to Believe in.

Something that gives their lives Meaning and Purpose.

Something that gives them a Reason to live.

Something giving them Love.

Something that gives them Honor.

Something that gives them Power.

Something that gives them Freedom.

Something that gives them Position.

These things can make them extremely susceptible and, therefore, freely choose to volunteer themselves to become captives.

THE STOCKHOLM SYNDROME

"The 'Stockholm Syndrome' is a proposed condition or theory that tries to explain why hostages sometimes develop a psychological bond with their captors...

Emotional bonds can form between captors and captives during intimate time together, but these are considered irrational by some in light of the danger or risk endured by the victims." [quoted from Wikipedia®]

We've observed Stockholm Syndrome scenarios play themselves out in actual hostage situations. Where captives were first imprisoned by their abductors—whether any part of it started out voluntarily. Then once realizing that they cannot escape; they end up going from hating and resisting their captors; to tolerating and existing under them; to becoming accustom to them; to becoming thankful to them; to embracing them; to cooperating with them; to eventually becoming them.

They start out 'Happy'

BELIEF SYSTEMS

DEFINITION OF BELIEF SYSTEMS

I'm not big into the philosophers, but since I'm not depending upon their beliefs to define our relationship to the True and Living God, I will use their definitions of Belief Systems here as a premise for this one subject.

"Belief systems are structured sets of principles or tenets held to be true by individuals or larger groups, encompassing aspects such as [or contain aspects such as] morality, life purpose, or empirical [pragmatic] reality.

They profoundly influence human behavior, shaping individual code of conduct, societal actions, values, and perceptions." - as quoted from HelpfulProfessor.com®

And their quote is from Uso-Domenech & Nescolarde-Selva ®, 2016, which also includes,

"In beliefs we live, we move and we are [...] the beliefs constitute the base of our life, the land on which we live [...] All our conduct, including the intellectual life, depends on the system of our authentic beliefs. In them [...] lies latent, as implications of whatever specifically we do or we think [...] the man, at heart, is believing or, which is equal, the deepest stratum of our life, the spirit that maintains and carries all the others, is formed by beliefs..." (as originally quoted from Ortega y Gasset ®)

People create and form *Belief Systems* around their needs, lacks, and desires, just as with the enticements described above. That (unfortunately) are easily exploitable by other people (and the demons behind them) wanting rule, power, and control. Men (and women) love power and control—as discussed in the first book.

FOR EXAMPLE: CATHOLICISM

Let's look at Catholicism as one example. While I have met some wonderful Catholic believers who have truly met the Lord, received Him into their lives, and some Spirit-filled, there are many who are only members of the denomination with no personal relationship with the Lord. Who live their lives by rote and religion.

It's easy for many onlookers to understand that worshipping Mary, the Saints, statues, and/or going about the numerous rituals of that religion are a *false Belief System* created by men (or of demons-in-nations).

HOW ABOUT MORMONISM?

The "prophet" Joseph Smith's many letters and the Book of Mormon, based on his "divine revelations" from "God," are meant to lead his followers to "greater knowledge" beyond the Bible.

Many of us recognize the Mormon religion as a cult that has swayed many. It's easy for many onlookers to understand the "divinely inspired" Book of Mormon is a *false Belief System* created by men (or of demons-in-nations).

HOW ABOUT MUSLIMS?

Have you ever met or listened to Muslims or Islamists—the staunch practitioners of their religion? Not those who have become Christian Believers.

Again, it's easy for many onlookers to understand that the Muslim religion, with its "divinely inspired" Quran, is quite extreme with all its constraints, beliefs, and forced actions on its followers. It's easy to see this is a *false Belief System* created by men (or of demons-in-nations).

HOW ABOUT OTHERS?

Would it surprise you to find out that many onlookers, disapproving of the religions above, being part of their denominations or religions, are just as deeply entrenched in their *false Belief Systems?*

You need to understand that many of those same people are "stuck" in very similar *Belief Systems.* They just dress theirs in more "spiritual" sounding definitions—but the same rote, rituals, and deceptions—the same demon/rulers over their nations; still bound in chains and weights they don't see. They are equally stuck. And whether obvious to them, they still need to be set free.

Many Christians, maybe even most, "float along" in life and have *NO [ZERO]* knowledge of the spiritual dilemma they live in. They're oblivious to what has transpired in their lives or the background behind them.

They go to church. Sing a few songs. Listen to the preacher / pastor /

minister / priest. Spend an hour of their week, then go home to just "live their lives." Then repeat the entire process again.

They do as they're told. Pay their tithes and obey the presets (rules) given. This, they're told, is what God wants. They're told if they do this, all will be good for them on earth and when they get to Heaven.

They go about their lives in oblivion. Just walking, living in rote.

Yet, deep down, they know something isn't right.

What's wrong?

After doing all I've been told to do, why do I still feel this way?

Deeply burdened.

Deeply saddened.

Unable to put a finger on it.

Nor can anyone else.

WHAT ARE BELIEF SYSTEMS?

Simply: *Belief Systems* in every religion, denomination, and the churches are the very essence, heart, and foundation of each. They're rooted in structured sets of laws, rules, doctrines, constructs, principles, tenets, limitations, and rituals that encompass *"their Beliefs"*, even if backed by scripture. They're taught, entrenched, required, commanded, and demanded in these old and/or new denominations, even if they call themselves "non-denominations". These *Belief Systems* are the very Heartbeat and held to be the *"Only Truth"* by these groups. Encompassing their *"divine understanding."* Their singular interpretation of scriptures. Their sense of right and wrong. Their life purpose. Their sole rational perspective shaping their understanding of Heaven and earth. These *Belief Systems* profoundly influence their behavior, their group code of conduct, their individual code of conduct, their societal actions, their values, and their perceptions. Which leave *NO* room to be challenged in any way or at any time by anyone.

Other Words used in Belief Systems

Let's look at some of the many words used in *Belief Systems:*

Cannon Law

Theology

Convictions

Ideology

Dogma

Church Doctrine

Holy Doctrine

Strick Doctrine

Orthodox Doctrine

Faith System

Teachings

Beliefs

Belief in God

Creed

Precepts

Liturgy

Rites

Ceremonies

Tenets

Tradition

Theological Tradition

Theological Notion

Theological Ideas

Theological Ideals

Practices

Sacrament

Ordinance

Religious Tenets

Religious Ceremony

Religious Tradition

Religious Belief

Religious Precept

Religious Principle

Religious View

Religious Concept

Religious Convictions

Religious Ethics

Religious Expression

Religious Myths

Religious Persuasion

Religious Thinking

Religious Thought

Devout Belief

Fervent Belief

Christian Belief

Christian Faith

Christian Principle

Procedures

Routines

Rituality

Rules

Norms

Rote

Dictates

Guidelines

Observations

Behaviors

Laws

Accepted Behaviors

"By the book"

"Established way of doing things"

"Our way of doing things"

"Dos and Don'ts"

ARE DOCTRINES GOOD OR BAD?

For now, let's group all these words together and call them doctrines. Since that's the term the scriptures use.

Doctrines are,

"A belief or set of beliefs, especially political or religious ones, that are taught and accepted by a particular group." [quoted from Dictionary.Cambridge.org®] and "A principle or position or the body of principles in a branch of knowledge or system of belief; something that is taught." [quoted from Merriam-Webster.com®]

So in simple terms, doctrines are principles, beliefs, or teachings.

Are some principles, beliefs, and teachings bad?

Are some principles, beliefs, and teachings good?

We will see with *false Belief Systems* there are bad doctrines, bad principles, bad beliefs, and bad teachings.

In Hebrews 13:9, we see,

"Do not be carried away by **Varied** and **Strange DOCTRINES, TEACHINGS,** and **INSTRUCTIONS**;"

In Ephesians 4:14, we see,

"As a result, we are no longer to be children, tossed here and there by waves and carried about by **EVERY WIND** of **DOCTRINE**, by the trickery of men, by craftiness in deceitful scheming;"

In Second Timothy 4:3-4, we see,

"For the time will come when they will not endure **SOUND DOCTRINE**; but **wanting** to have their **ears tickled**, they will **accumulate** for themselves **teachers** in **accordance** to their **own desires**, and will **turn away** their ears from the **Truth** and will turn aside to **Myths**."

And in First Timothy 6:3-4, we see,

"If anyone advocates *a* **DIFFERENT DOCTRINE** and does not agree with **SOUND WORDS**, those of our **Lord Jesus Christ**, and with the **Doctrine Conforming** to **Godliness**,

He is conceited and understands nothing; but he has a morbid interest in controversial questions and disputes about words, out of which arise envy, strife, abusive language, evil suspicions."

So the questions remain: Can there be good doctrines? Good principles? Good beliefs? Good teachings?

YES.

In Titus 1:9, we see,

"Holding fast the **FAITHFUL WORD** which is in accordance with the teaching, so that he will be able both to exhort in **SOUND DOCTRINE** and to refute those who contradict."

In Titus 2:7-8, we see,

"In all things show yourself to be an example of good deeds, with **PURITY** in **DOCTRINE**, dignified, sound in speech which is beyond reproach, so that the opponent will be put to shame, having nothing bad to say about us."

In First Timothy 4:6, we see,

"In pointing out these things to the brethren, you will be a good servant of **Christ (the Anointing)** Jesus, constantly nourished on the **WORDS** of the **FAITH** and of the **SOUND DOCTRINE** which you have been following."

In Titus 2:1, we see,

"BUT [as for] you, **TEACH** what is **Fitting** and **Becoming** to **Sound** (wholesome) **DOCTRINE** [the character and right living that identify true Christians]."

And in Titus 1:9, we see,

"He must hold fast to the **Sure** and **Trustworthy Word** of **God** as he was taught it, so that he maybe able both to give **Stimulating Instruction** and **Encouragement** in **Sound** (wholesome) **DOCTRINE** and to **Refute** and **Convict** those who **Contradict** and **Oppose** it [showing the wayward their error]."

What's the Distinction between them?

The distinction is in the **FAITHFUL WORD** of **God** versus teachings of men and/or demons. The **FAITHFUL WORD** [the written, and the Spoken, Word of the Living God] are **SOUND DOCTRINE**. That's **PURITY** in **DOCTRINE**.

Then you might argue: But the foundation of our religion or denomination began with the Purity of the Word. You might be right. But the question remains: Did that Purity (of the Word) get tainted over time? Distorted? Enshrined in precepts, tenants, and rules of men to become false teachings of men and demons? No matter how few or many degrees off.

If so, what went wrong?

The Church of No Tangents

We used to make a joke about "The Church of No Tangents."

We wanted a church that would always remain faithful, focused, and true to the Lord. A church that would *NEVER* mess up, *NEVER* miss the Lord, *NEVER* miss the mark, *NEVER* go off course, and could *NEVER* be fooled into doing so. *NEVER* fall for religions. *NEVER* fall for denominations. *NEVER* fall for any deceptions from the enemy. Therefore, we decided to create "The Church of No Tangents."

To accomplish this goal, we discussed how we could achieve that perfect place of no tangents. We were determined to *NEVER* go on tangents. Matter of fact, because we hated tangents so much, we planned on exposing every possible tangent imaginable—*ALL* the time—in every way. We planned on calling out, defining, and labeling each one. We planned on discussing each one in detail. We intended to preach about them. Our plan was to cover all of them during our teaching times.

We planned on creating rules, tenants, and precepts so that we'd *NEVER* fall for them—*EVER*. We planned on creating ways to stay accountable to each other so no one would *EVER* fall for a tangent. And we planned on instructing *ALL* new converts of these same truths.

How does that sound?

Does it sound like a good plan?

Does it sound like we'd NEVER mess up?

Think again.

Did you figure out the point of this analogy?

To make sure we didn't go on any tangents, we were going on a *MAJOR* tangent to do so. Our planned new church was already a failure. We did exactly what we said we didn't want to do.

Therefore, can you see how *EVERY Belief System* that man has ever created, adopted, or embraced was inherently doomed to fail from the beginning?

Rulers Over Denominations

Do you remember the definition of denominations from my first book, where denomination is a "demon-in-a-nation"? And denominations are "demons-in-nations"? Ruling over God's people in the churches.

Just as the messenger angel told Daniel (in Daniel 10:20),

"I shall now return to fight against the prince of Persia; and the prince of Greece"—these being some of the demon rulers over earthly kingdoms of the past—that Michael and his warrior angels were fighting in Old Testament times,

whereas nowadays,

"For we are not wrestling with flesh and blood [contending only with physical opponents], but against the despotisms [tyranny, absolute power or authority], against the powers, against [the master spirits who are] the world rulers of this present darkness, against the spirit forces of wickedness in the heavenly (supernatural) sphere" (Ephesians 6:12),

these are the demon rulers, tyrants, master spirits, world rulers, spirit forces of wickedness presiding over the "demons-in-nations"—who want to dominate us in New Testament times.

Resulting in and backing the *ungodly Belief Systems* that rule many, many churches today.

Just like in the Stockholm Syndrome, good people, God's people, wanting to find Him, unfortunately start out by being taken hostage by *Belief Systems* and their rulers—men and women (leaders) deceived by ungodly spirits—the spirit of the antichrist. Maybe some of these people can feel [recognize] that something is *"OFF"*—like a *"CHECK in their spirit"*—but they surrender their will to the leaders backed by these demons-in-nations.

Drawn in because of the *ENTICEMENTS* (above) at work in their lives.

As told in First John 4:1-3,

"Beloved, do *NOT* put faith in every spirit, but prove (test) the spirits to discover whether they proceed from God; for **many false prophets** have gone forth into the world.

By this you may know (perceive and recognize) the Spirit of God: every spirit which acknowledges and confesses [the fact] that Jesus **Christ** *(the Anointing)* [actually] has become man and has come in the flesh is of God [has God for its source];

And every spirit which does not acknowledge and confess that Jesus **Christ** *(the* **Anointing***)* has come in the flesh [but would annul, destroy, sever, disunite Him] is not of God [does not proceed from Him]. This [non-confession] is the *[spirit] of the* **antichrist**, [of] which you heard that it was coming, and now it is already in the world."

You might say, "We're too savvy to fall for that. We've asked the Lord into our lives and we'd *NEVER* fall for such."

Unfortunately, many would be wrong.

Both Paul and John Warn Us

In Second Corinthians 11:3-4,

"But [now] I am fearful, lest that even as the serpent **beguiled** *[deceived]* Eve by his cunning [and craftiness], so **your minds** may be **corrupted**, **seduced**, and **led astray** from the **simplicity** and **wholehearted**, **sincere** and **pure devotion** to **Christ** *[the Anointing]*.

For [you seem readily to endure it] if a **man comes** and **preaches** another Jesus than the one we preached, or if **you receive** a **different spirit** from the *[Spirit]* you [once] **received** or a **different gospel** from the one you [then] received and welcomed [being a different gospel which you have not

34

accepted];"

Paul's warning us to be on the watch, on the ready, on the lookout for those who will try to deceive us. Men who will preach and teach *"another [different] gospel"*, *"another [different] spirit"* according to the spirit of the antichrist that rule [behind] them. *False Belief Systems* that entrap Believers. Taking them away from the *"simplicity* and *wholehearted, sincere* and *pure devotion* to *Christ [the Anointing]."*

And in Second John 9,

"Anyone who runs on ahead [of God] and does *NOT abide* in the *DOCTRINE* (Teaching) of *Christ (the Anointing)* [who is not content with what He taught] does *NOT* have *God;* but he who *continues* to *live* in the *DOCTRINE* (Teaching) of *Christ (the Anointing)* [does have God], he has *both* the *Father* and the *Son."*

Once again, *Christ (the Anointing),* as taught from the first book, is the basis of *ALL Sound* and *True DOCTRINE.* Any variance from teaching *Christ (the Anointing)* is the basis of *false Belief Systems.*

Could The Good News Become Bad News?

Many succumb to these *false Belief Systems* simply by the influence of those who brought you the Good News—unfortunately tainted with a mixture of Truth and Lies.

You say, "How's that?"

"Wouldn't God protect us from such?"

Maybe, if we truly had learned how to yield and walk with the Lord, as taught in the first book.

But unfortunately, again, for the rest under the influence of many churches of the past, present, and future ruled by leaders under those false spirits, will not. These are ones filled with *"Mixed Unholy Fires",* which we will address a little later.

Continuing on, these same good people, remaining under the leadership of these demons-in-nations, will after a while, get used to the *"Mixed Unholy Fires"* that are being entrenched deep inside them—learning to ignore the *"OFF"* feelings. The longer they remain, they will accept all of this as *"The Normal"*. Then they will accept it as *"The Right Thing"*. Eventually they will accept it as *"The Best Thing"*. At which time they will become zealots *EXPECTING ALL* others should have it and therefore need to go through the same (unholy) process to achieve the same *"Excellent State of Spirituality"* they've achieved. A state of consciousness that *NO* one can achieve except by undergoing and submitting to that process.

Remind you of anything?

Maybe Stockholm syndrome?

When that level of indoctrination by men, women, and ungodly spirits has matured, then their (spiritual) captors have recreated them in their image. Fully enveloped, it now becomes time for them to go and do the same and *"procreate"* in the exact same way. Therefore, they will go find and take new hostages to start the whole Stockholm Syndrome process over again. First as trusted helpers to their indoctrinators. Eventually to become the new leaders in those churches or some new church planting elsewhere—as the new indoctrinators absolutely believing in and strongly promoting their one and only true *"cause"* and *"beliefs"*.

This will repeat over and over and over again, furthering their *false Belief Systems* under their "demons-in-nations".

As they begin to feel the bonds, sadness sets in

BELIEF SYSTEMS VERSUS BELIEVING - IS THERE A DIFFERENCE?

YES! A BIG DIFFERENCE!

We're told to **BELIEVE** all throughout the scriptures.

You might say, "I don't see the difference."

We just discussed *Belief Systems* and we see what they are. So, what's the difference?

If you read the first book, there's a chapter in it called, "REAL FAITH, TRUE FAITH". Inside is a very clear definition of what true believing is in full. But for here, in short, we will mention that actual believing is a living, active, true, unequivocal walk of faith with the Father; within the four corners of His Word and by His Peace that passes understanding. If you didn't read it yet, you need to stop and do so.

When living in that true and real place of faith, actively seeing and responding to the Helper, the Spirit of God, we will do as the Father is doing and speak as the Father is saying, as our Big Brother, Jesus, did while on the earth.

THAT'S THE POLAR OPPOSITE OF BELIEF SYSTEMS.

Do you see the difference?

Belief Systems, whether positive or negative, represent humanity's efforts to quantify God and impose manufactured frameworks and constructs on their adherents. Whereas actual believing is a true, active, and living relationship.

THEY ARE NOT EQUAL IN ANY WAY, FORM, SHAPE, OR REALITY.

[THESE] BELIEF SYSTEMS ARE CULTS

Let's define cults. Cults are,

1. A religion regarded as unorthodox or spurious [outwardly similar or corresponding to something without having its genuine qualities : false]. Also : its body of adherents.

2. Great devotion to a person, idea, object, movement, or work. Especially : such devotion regarded as a literary or intellectual fad. The object of such devotion. Usually a small group of people characterized by such devotion.

3. A system of religious beliefs and ritual. Also : its body of adherents.

4. Formal religious veneration [respect or awe inspired by the dignity, wisdom, dedication, or talent of a person] : WORSHIP.

5. A system for the cure of disease based on dogma set forth by its promulgator [a person or people who announce a law as a way of putting it into execution]. This is typically attributed to a health cult.

[As quoted from the Merriam Webster Dictionary® online.]

Let's look at each of these attributes.

Number 1 summarized states, "A religion regarded as unorthodox or false, including its body of adherents [those who follow or uphold a leader, party, cause, opinion, or the like; a follower, partizan, or supporter]."

You go, "I got you now." I saw the words "unorthodox" and "false". And I can tell you I belong to a religion or denomination that has existed "forever," is totally accepted as the "norm," and is the opposite of "false."

Oh no, did you just blow up my argument?

Nope.

Why not?

Just because many people accept things as "normal" and not "false", does *NOT* make them so. Just because demons-in-nations have been ruling those religions and denominations "forever", does *NOT* make them correct or right.

They could be a cult.

Number 2 summarized states, "Great devotion to a person, idea, object, movement, or work. Especially, such devotion regarded on an intellectual level. Usually, a group of people characterized by such devotion." Well, that sure sounds like *Belief Systems* we've been discussing.

Number 3 summarized states, "A system of religious beliefs and ritual. Also : its body of adherents [those who follow or uphold a leader, party, cause, opinion, or the like; a follower, partizan, or supporter]." Again, that sure sounds like *Belief Systems* we've been discussing.

Number 4 summarized states, "Formal religious veneration [respect or awe inspired by the dignity, wisdom, dedication, or talent of a person, persons, rulers or leaders] : WORSHIP [of the system or belief system]." And again, that sure sounds like *Belief Systems* we've been discussing.

Number 5 summarized states, "A system for the cure of (disease) based on dogma set forth by its promulgator [a person, persons, rulers, leaders who announce laws, rules, precepts, canon, beliefs, doctrine as a way of putting it into execution], typically attributed to a health cult." But what if it wasn't specifically a physical health cult? What if it was a mental or spiritual health cult? Or both? And again, that sure sounds like *Belief Systems* we've been discussing.

Can you now see why these *Belief Systems* are cults? Even possibly in the greatest and oldest of religions.

So, are all Belief Systems cults?

No.

But they can be.

WHAT ARE MIXED UNHOLY STRANGE FIRES?

In Leviticus 10:1-3 we see,

"Now Nadab and Abihu, the sons of Aaron, took their respective firepans, and after putting fire in them, placed incense on it and offered Strange Fire before the LORD, which He had not commanded them.

And fire came out from the Presence of the LORD and consumed them, and they died before the LORD.

Then Moses said to Aaron, it is what the LORD spoke, saying, 'by those who come near Me I will be treated as Holy, and before all the people I will be Honored.'"

You need to note here that this *Mixed Unholy Strange Fire* came from the "Priests of God"—from the highest leaders in Israel. It happened when they thought they were doing something *BETTER* for God by mixing incense on top of God's pure fire (His Pure Word).

Does God want something *BETTER* than *His Spirit* coming out of men or women (or the demons and ungodly spirits behind them)?

NO!

This should be a resounding warning that God's people, even the leaders of churches, as the "Priests of God", may mix in Strange and Unholy things with the Purity of God's Word, thereby creating and releasing *Mixed Unholy Strange Fire.*

Unfortunately, it can even be leaders in His Church, The Church, not just in the churches (denominations or not). As well as, it can be any of God's people who are supposed to be yielded Believers [the elect] who have *Mixed Incense* from themselves, other people, other things, or other *'gods'* into His Pure Fire and then try to present these things as Pure.

But they are NOT.

REMEMBER LEADERS LOVE POWER?

Do you remember from the first book about how *MANY* leaders want and love Power? How that's a gateway to failure?

Always remember this truism "that people love Power." And the devil, who fell from Heaven with the same delusions of grandeur, loves to play that game on them to lead them down the wrong path.

As the old saying goes, "Power corrupts, and absolute power corrupts absolutely." (Lord Acton, nineteenth-century British politician)

So men and women who want Power will (gladly) remain under their demons-in-nations' *false Belief Systems* to maintain that Power.

Is This True for All Denominations and Religions?

YES.

Are Some Worse Than Others?

YES.

Is This True for All Churches and All Believers?

NO.

But don't think you're off the hook just yet. This is not a "get out of jail free card."

Opposite of how you might think, those who are closer to reaching the Spirit of God, the more Spirit-filled, the *WORSE* it'll be. Because the spirit of the antichrist will come against them the hardest to make sure that they cannot reach their full potential with the Lord—to learn how to Walk in Truth with the Father—then stop the enemy's plans [per the first book].

Does that mean *ALL* of God's people in those denominations, religions, and churches are under the influence of unholy gods?

NO.

But could there be many?

MOST LIKELY.

So assume nothing. Yield yourself to the Lord and let the Spirit of God do the evaluation in you. You cannot do that evaluation yourself. Others cannot do it for you either.

How about Believers who are not part of denominations?

How about churches that specifically are non-denominational?

How about those who've left the churches for those same or other reasons?

Can it happen to any of them?

SURE.

You don't need a label to be under the influence of ungodly spirits.

Then, can anyone break free from these *Belief Systems?*

ABSOLUTELY.

But, most likely, none of us *EVER* started free of them, no matter what you might believe. And, if we want freedom, it will cost us a steep price to get it. If God's people want and choose to be free of *these Belief Systems,* then they must go into the wilderness, for as long as it takes, and allow the Spirit of God to do everything necessary in them to **Set Them Free**.

There's no CHEAP alternative.

There's no quick way around it.

After God's people leave their places of bondage, they must learn to walk **FREE** in Him. We'll learn how, so stay tuned.

WHY PEOPLE HOLD ON TO BELIEF SYSTEMS

When they realize there's 'no escape' anguish sets in

People hold on to *Belief Systems* because they think "they're safe." Not just because leaders told them "to do them."

What does "safe" mean to them?

It, again, has a double meaning. First, they think their *Belief Systems* are "safe" versus the rest of the "craziness out there." Second, they think the *Belief Systems* keep them "safe" from the "craziness out there." At least, that's how they were indoctrinated with the "cool-aid" they freely drank.

Therefore, the "buy in."

An outside example: As a person who has some level of OCD and germaphobia, I can definitely relate in that way. I know no one else has any such deficiencies but me—but just to inform those who don't, these mental challenges can not only be draining on me, but those around me.

As a (low-level) OCD, I need to see some things done in a particular way or else I may not accept the work or the results as correct. As a (mid-level) germaphobe I feel that if I don't wash or disinfect my hands all the time, as well as, everything purchased from stores to eliminate germs, I'll get the transfer of said germs from those products on myself or my loved ones.

While there is certainly some truth in this premise, the fact that I must disinfect the milk container before using it can be a bit much. My wife is not that way and she doesn't get sick. As she says, maybe her body has built up the resistance to the germs by not disinfecting everything.

She just might be right.

So why do I do all the above?

Because it makes me "feel safe."

Get the analogy yet?

What makes you feel "safe"?

Is it a nice car? A nice house? A nice job? Enough money in the bank?

Enough in savings? Enough investments? How about having sufficient health insurance or life insurance? What other things can you think of that make you feel "safe"?

None of those things are bad in themselves. But what are you willing to sacrifice to get that "safe" feeling? And, if that's true for physical things, then can you see why we easily fall for such in "spiritual things?"

For that very reason alone, is why we're so easily deceived (duped) into falling for these *false Belief Systems* and willing to "pay the price", whatever it is, to get that "safe" feeling.

Now, can you begin to grasp and understand the plot and ploy of the enemy behind all these things? And why we fall for them?

WHAT ARE THE "OFF" FEELINGS ABOVE?

What is the *"CHECK in the spirit"* we can feel?

All of them are *WARNINGS* from the Holy Spirit inside *(ALL of)* us, as Believers. Trying to keep us from falling for the *Mixed Unholy Strange Fires* that come from the "Priests of God" and their [Stockholm Syndrome] converts in the demons-in-nations.

It's this same **Spirit of God** *(the **Anointing**)* as discussed in great detail in the first book. Where we learned, we must yield ourselves to Him to have the Peace of God that can lead and guide us from the *false Belief Systems* into His Truth.

"And the Peace of God, which surpasses all understanding [comprehension], will guard your hearts and your minds in **Christ** *[the* **Anointing***]* Jesus." (Philippians 4:7)

We need to learn to operate in and live by *The Peace* that passes understanding. When we stop and yield our hearts to the Father, He will give us His Peace in the best and worst of times.

So how do we distinguish which is God's still small voice versus the enemy's tangents and deceptions?

By HIS PEACE, that PASSES UNDERSTANDING.

We can learn how to tell them apart by knowing God's Word, then sensing if God's Peace that passes understanding is there or not. But remember, the enemy knows God's Word better than us, so the Word by itself is not enough.

LAYERS AND LAYERS OF THE ONION

Belief Systems and our *Stockholm indoctrinations* have many, many layers. Years and experiences—good and bad—have built them as an onion around us, layer by layer by layer. Unfortunately, we cannot fully understand nor undo the layers by ourselves.

Therefore, just as it took many years to build them, it may take many years to undo them. Stay tuned to learn how God's loving process of the wilderness will accomplish this.

THE GOOD NEWS

Now that I've painted the very dim picture that *ALL* of us have most likely fallen victim to ungodly spirits, ungodly or false leaders, ungodly churches (denominations or not)—*ALL* received *Unholy Mixtures* in us—let me tell you there's truly *Good News* available to God's people.

WE ALL CAN BE SET FREE.

We **ALL** can learn to live outside *false Belief Systems.*

We **ALL** can learn how to live in and out of the ***Presence*** *of* ***God.***

All of this to be discussed later.

CHAPTER FOUR

TYPES OF CAPTIVITY

THE NUMBER ONE TYPE IS BELIEF SYSTEMS

A s we just spent a full chapter discussing *Belief Systems*, it's the first, foremost, and probably the greatest type of captivity that encumbers and defeats God's people.

Guaranteed: If we don't get out from under those *Belief Systems*, then we're held and will remain captive.

AND, OF COURSE, THERE ARE THE AREAS OF CAPTIVITY

As discussed in the chapter "AREAS OF CAPTIVITY", there are many areas of thought that hold us captive.

OPPRESSION AND POSSESSION

One area we did not expand upon in that chapter was oppression and possession.

As mentioned, the first book covered oppression and possession in great detail. If you didn't read it yet, stop here and do that so you can better understand what I'm about to say next.

There are many [evil] spirits that can oppress or possess us. It actually doesn't matter which kind it is. If we've given them the rights [permission] to do either—the effects on us will be the same. Us being held captive. Unable to be free from their tyranny (without God's intervention).

The Four Ways These Spirits Keep Us Captive

First, from oppression. As clearly defined in greater detail in the first book, oppression is when we allow [evil] spirits to attach themselves to us [permanently] to influence us, torture us, hold us captive from the outside in. Somewhere along the way, we agreed to the attachment—so the spirits will tyrannize us, as they like, as long as they like, and at will.

Second, from possession. As clearly defined in greater detail in the first book, possession is when we allow [evil] spirits to live in us [permanently] to influence us, torture us, hold us captive from the inside out. Somewhere along the way, we agreed to the possession—so, again, the spirits will tyrannize us, as they like, as long as they like, and at will.

Third, from ourselves [our old nature, our old man, the flesh] working in agreement with either oppression or possession, in an active relationship. Meaning, while in the state of being oppressed or possessed, we willingly work in concert with them.

Or fourth, from ourselves [our old nature, our old man, the flesh] working in agreement with either oppression or possession, in an inactive relationship. Meaning, even though we are free from the spirits' oppression or possession, we still choose to cooperate with their evil influences.

Note: If we're active in the fourth way, it's just a matter of time before we'll get oppressed or possessed again by those same spirits, plus seven times more and worse than the originals. Read the first book for clarity.

Let's Talk About Some of The Spirits That Can Rule Us and Hold Us Captive

This is not an exhaustive list, by any means. But here are some of the spirits that can haunt and tyrannize our lives.

A religious spirit.

A spirit of self-righteousness.

A spirit of spirituality.

A spirit of witchcraft.

A spirit of rebellion.

A spirit of lust.

A spirit of hate.

A spirit of anger.

A spirit of wrath.

A spirit of murder.

A malevolent spirit.

A malicious spirit.

A disruptive spirit.

A lying spirit.

A spirit of fear.

A paralyzing spirit.

A spirit of deception.

An anxious spirit.

A spirit of depression.

A spirit of infirmity.

A spirit of loathing [others].

A spirit of self-loathing.

A spirit of judgement.

A spirit of unforgiveness.

A spirit of pride.

And many others—too many to name. But if you can think of any type of evil or any of the self-indulged or mental areas that could influence you, you can believe there's an [evil] spirit behind them.

Let's Take One Spirit as an Example to See What It's Done to Us

While we could look at many on the "evil" side that might be much more obvious, let's look at a religious spirit that lives in or around *MANY* in the churches that might not be so obvious.

A religious spirit is actually very similar and many times works in conjunction with a spirit of spirituality, a spirit of self-righteousness, and a spirit of judgement. These individual or combined spirits control Believers to remain in captivity in the churches and *false Belief Systems.* Those with this spirit or spirits will many times receive accolades from their fellow

Stockholm inductees for their great religiousness, revelation, discernment, and spirituality—emboldening them all the more.

When a religious spirit rules someone, they feel empowered. They feel they have the spiritual "right" and moral "obligation" from God, and are therefore "ordained", to judge others outside their *Belief Systems* and/or what they deem to be acceptable speech, dress, words, or actions. And they do so with moral superiority. Unfortunately, they were ordained by *"god"*, he with the little "g".

Do you remember the right kinds of judgement versus the singular wrong kind of judgement expanded upon in the first book? There's an entire chapter on "JUDGMENT" where we can see there's only one kind of judgement we're not allowed to do. Where we judge others or what they do from God's white-throne character judgement.

The Greek has numerous words for judgement that we're allowed and should do. That chapter defines many. We're allowed to judge if it's discernment, examining ourselves, deciding between right and wrong, distinguishing good from evil, and being exposed by the light and the truth.

The judgement we're instructed not to do is "Judge not, lest you be judged" from the book of Matthew. This *judgement* is the Greek word, 'krinō' (kree-no), which means to *"act as judge," "condemn," "pass judgement," "as to law," "stand trial."*

We see the same word 'krinō' used in Revelations 20:11-12's Great White Throne Judgement, where God will judge all of us for eternity.

Yet, when someone is under the influence of a religious spirit, whether working in conjunction with a self-righteousness spirit and/or a spirit of spirituality, they believe they've been given the clear directive from God to judge others ('krinō' them) and expel them for their heretical words, actions, or teachings. Again, read that chapter in the first book to get clarity about when the religious believe they're allowed to expel others.

Once again, BS.

When I wrote the first book, I had several early readers, before publishing, who stumbled over me using what they defined as "foul language" from time-to-time throughout the book. Where I honestly was just giving my raw exposé of my life as I grew in the Lord—the good, the bad, and the ugly. Yet, to the contrary, I had many more that did not.

After publication, some early launch team readers and reviewers gave me similar feedback. One Christian sister told me she could not leave a review for me for *ANY* of the *GOOD* things I'd written in the book because of the use of such language *ANYWHERE* in the book—no matter how slight. She said if she left a review, she'd have to rate it very low and word the review badly for the reason of that language.

This was after I'd read her book and left her a wonderful 5-star review, despite not agreeing 100 percent with all her content. Why did I leave the 5-star review? Because I didn't let the little things I may've disagreed with ruin the 98 percent great content she was writing about.

I'd asked the Lord repeatedly during the twenty plus times I edited the first book, "Should I remove the foul language my early readers were identifying? Should I replace it with dumbed down, toned down words no one would stumble on?" I never heard I was to do such in all those times. Instead, I had His Peace that passes understanding to leave it as it was. So, I left them in as part of my "raw exposé."

It wasn't until writing this book and remembering what my one reviewer (above) had said that the Lord told me He wanted me to keep the foul language in the first book. Not only because it was my raw exposé, but also to reveal those who have a religious spirit when they read it. And to challenge them to repent and come out of captivity.

Another Side of That Same Spirit is Sacrilegiousness

The other day my wife and I took our 12-year-old daughter to her friend's birthday party. They had a DJ. The birthday girl, our daughter, and friends were dancing away and singing to the assorted music played. One song they wanted repeated over and over again was "Church Clap" [Copyright by KB and Lecrae (Christian Hip-Hop artists)].

I admit I'm not into Hip-Hop, so the song and lyrics "hit me the wrong way." It's definitely not my "cup of tea" [normal] kind of worship music. But later at home, the Lord convinced me to look up the lyrics and listen to it again. Which I did.

I was wrong.

This song is just an expression of their commitment to the Lord. It's their way of reaching out too many in a format that young people love. It was allowing a great value to be instilled deep inside of them as they danced and sang along.

Is this sacrilegious?

Sacrilegious means "Extremely disrespectful towards something considered sacred. An action that causes deep offense to a believer." [quoted from Vocabulary.com®] or "Treating something holy or important without respect." [quoted from Dictionary.Cambridge.org®]

Unknowingly, I was internally judging this as sacrilegious—what I would judge was not pleasing to the Lord. Things I think would offend the Lord, because [in that moment] they offended me.

What is sacrilegiousness?

What do we judge as sacrilegious?

Why do we think we can judge anything as sacrilegious?

What kind of judgement are we doing when we judge something as sacrilegious?

Again, unfortunately, this is the judgement we're told not to do, 'krinō'.

When any of us are judging people or the things they do as sacrilegious, it's 'krinō'ing them—judging their character. And from God's perspective, it's not allowed—*EVER*.

Not only is judging sacrilegiousness wrong, but isn't it just another extension of a religious spirit?

Isn't it just fake religiosity?

Isn't it just fake spirituality?

YES, YES, and YES.

I didn't realize that I was allowing a religious spirit to influence me. But I was. And just as I fell for the deception, many others do too in their own ways.

We need to reject religious spirits and all other spirits from the *god* of this world.

Guaranteed: If we don't get out from under all those "Areas of Captivity", then we're held and will remain captive.

NOW LET'S DISCUSS SOME OTHERS

~

UNDER THE WEIGHT OF SIN

The question is *NOT,* "Do we sin?"

The real question is, "Do we allow sins to remain, fester, and rule our lives?"

WHAT IS SIN?

When we think about *SIN,* we think of the normal "things that will take us down" (more fully defined in the first book). Maybe like,

Pride.

Power.

Ego.

Control.

Lust.

(Misuse of) Sex.

(Worshipping) Money.

Anger, Hate, Wrath.

Falling for "religion" or religiosity (false religions).

Or the opposite—no religion (remembering that *TRUE RELIGION* is looking after orphans and widows [James 1:27]).

Falling for anything that will take our eyes off the Lord.

While all those are *sins,* the correct definition of *SIN* is anything that takes us out of *fellowship* and in a *relationship* with the Father, as my best friend, Chuck, says all the time.

In Isaiah 59:2 we see,

"But your iniquities have made a **SEPARATION** between you and your God, and your sins have hidden His face from you, so that He will not hear."

Now that we can see the difference between *SIN* and *sins,* let's get something straight right here, for now and forever [for as long as we're living on the earth]—it's not about being "perfect"—none of us can *EVER* be "perfect." There was and is *ONLY* one who was *EVER* perfect on earth and that was Jesus, alone.

Yet, you might want to argue that statement by quoting Matthew 5:48, where Jesus told us,

"Therefore, you are to be ***Perfect***, as your heavenly Father is ***Perfect***."

Wow!

Guess you'd conclude that I don't know what I'm talking about now.

Right?

Because if Jesus told us to be ***Perfect***, then it sure sounds like it *MUST* be possible. Therefore, there *MUST* be a way that we can somehow live a "perfect" sin-free life.

Have you ever tried doing that?

I have.

It's exhausting.

Know why?

Because it's IMPOSSIBLE!

Let's look a little deeper. Matthew 5:48 in the AMP version reads:

"You, therefore, must be ***Perfect*** [GROWING into ***complete maturity*** of godliness in ***mind*** and ***character***, having reached the proper height of virtue and integrity], as your heavenly Father is ***Perfect***."

The word ***Perfect*** in the Greek is 'teleios' (TEH-lei-os), meaning "***having reached its end***," "*i.e., 'complete', by extension, 'perfect',*" "***mature***," "*more perfect*," from the root word 'telos' (TEH-los) which means "***an end***," "*continually*," "*[until it's]* ***finished***," "*[until it's reached its intended]* *fulfillment,*" "*[until it's reached its intended]* **goal**," "*[until it's reached its intended]* **outcome**."

Doesn't that sound a lot like the process of **Sanctification** we discussed above? It's a lifelong process—here on earth—never ending; until it's reached its intended "*fulfillment,*" "*goal,*" "*outcome,*" and "*end.*"

Remember, "the earth is a testing ground."

Philippians 3:12-15 tells us,

"**NOT** that I have now **attained** [this ideal], or have already been made **Perfect**, but I press on to lay hold of (grasp) and make my own, that for which **Christ [the Anointing]** Jesus has laid hold of me and made me His own.

I do not consider, brethren, that I have captured and made it my own [**yet**]; but one thing I do [it is my one aspiration]: **forgetting** what lies **behind** and **straining forward** to what lies **ahead**,

I press on toward the goal to win the [supreme and heavenly] prize to which God in **Christ [the Anointing]** Jesus **is calling** us upward.

So let those [of us] who are **spiritually mature** and **full-grown** have this mind and hold these convictions; and if in any respect you have a different attitude of mind, God will make that clear to you also."

So, let's garner this same mind—it's about seeking, yielding, believing, and walking with the Lord [or allowing Him to walk with us] throughout this life. Let us learn to **focus on Him** versus the *SIN or sins*—knowing that *SIN* separates us from the Father. That separation alone—losing His Presence, His Anointing, His Peace—should be sufficient impetus to repent, to make a 180-degree turn from the sins that separate us, turning towards Him and return.

Guaranteed: If we don't get out from under the rule of *SIN*, then we're held and will remain captive.

THINKING THEY'RE SO SPIRITUAL

People, maybe Christians, maybe Believers, maybe the Saints, maybe the elect—some you may know—thinking they're so spiritual they hear from God, clearly, and all the time; and no one can tell them otherwise.

Have you ever met such Christians?

Are you one?

It's pretty hard to get through to those who are so "spiritually minded", who think they hear from *"god"* and can't be told anything to the contrary. They'll argue, until they're blue in the face, that you're wrong and they're right. Most, no actually *ALL*, who take that position simply are *WRONG*. They are hearing from *"god"*, he with the little "g", the *god* of this world or his rulers, cohorts, and demons.

Do you remember the scripture and discussion above, that we only "see, hear, and know in part?"

At *BEST* we see through a mirror (or a glass) dimly. At *BEST* we see, hear, and know in riddles, mysteries, obscurities, and enigmas. Therefore, anyone who says otherwise is *DECEIVED*.

NO one sees clearly. *NO* one hears perfectly. *NO* one knows all. Me included.

This is one of the great fallacies that will F— up those who pursue the spiritual realm. The devil knows it and he loves to play this game on Christians, Believers, the Saints, the elect. How much better than to deceive the Saints to believe they've got a direct pipeline to *"god"* that's better than anyone else does? Oh, the pride in that! Delivered by the *"god of pride"*.

Thinking, believing they're just a little (or a lot) better, then everyone else—that they're special envoys, prophets, watchmen (or women) for "god"—that they hear just a little (or a lot) better. Such makes them feel (extra) special, (extra) called, (extra) powerful—almost invincible. Note: There are true prophets from God and there are false prophets from the spirit of the antichrist [I explain the *BIG* differences in the first book, so I won't repeat it here].

It's hard to break that mind, heart, mental, and emotional *Belief System's* power that rules over such people. And, if so deceived, why would they ever listen or believe that they could be wrong and want to give that up?

It can only happen if and when they humble themselves before God, He with the Big "G". It can only happen when they want the Truth over that self-centered, self-satisfying, self-indulged, special new self-image as *"god's"* messengers—the power it brings—and the accolades from other self-indulged followers.

Guaranteed: If we don't get out from under that deception, then we're held and will remain captive.

UNDER THE WEIGHT OF "MANY DISTRACTIONS"

We learned in the first book many, many different distractions the enemy uses to encumber God's people.

Distractions on every side, even valid ones—ones that will try to keep your eyes focused away from the Lord.

Such as gaslit distractions in the churches:

Power.

Ego.

Control.

Fear.

Willing to do anything to gain acceptance.

Spirit-filled versus non-Spirit-filled.

Religiosity.

Fake spirituality.

Being under men's (or women's) authority.

Fake faith.

Judgements, wrong praying, etc.

Or gaslit distractions in our lives:

Temptation of every type of sin.

Fear.

Power.

Ego.

Control.

Money.

And many others.

Of course, there are legitimate things we can and/or must do in life, but many of these same things can distract us from putting the Lord first.

All the unhealthy distractions noted here, and others, will disable us from walking closely with the Lord.

Guaranteed: If we don't get out from under the control of those distractions, then we're held and will remain captive.

CAPTIVE IN OUR OWN THOUGHTS AND MINDS

We've been talking a lot about many areas of the mind and the thoughts that pass through it. The ruler of this world, who instilled in us from the beginning, our old nature, the old man, the flesh, trained us to listen to him. He trained our thought processes to *ALWAYS* fall back into his way of thinking—to be totally open to hearing from him and his wrong spirits. He engrained his thought patterns in us—therefore, he can *ALWAYS* control us—unless we allow God to intervene.

Remember, he's the prince of the power of the air.

Guaranteed: If we don't get out from under those thought patterns, then we're held and will remain captive.

EXPECTATIONS—WE'VE BEEN SETUP

The *god* of this world has set us up to live in captivity under the weight of expectations. The expectations of others, and even worse, our self-imposed expectations, weigh heavily on us. Expectations of what the world and the *god* of this world have taught us to accept as "the normal." Our beliefs dictate what we think God demands of us.

Unfortunately, none of these expectations are from our loving Father—they're a plot to take us down—away from the intimate relationship with God.

UNDER GUILT

This is a **BIG ONE**. Here the enemy has taught us, groomed us (and everyone else on earth) from the beginning, that if we cannot live up to these *Belief Systems,* and even worse, if we cannot live up to a *"SIN-FREE LIFE"*—then we will live under the *PENALTY* of *GUILT.* And we know we deserve it.

I'm not good enough.

No one would love or accept me if they only knew.

I know I don't accept myself.

Therefore, I'm sure God doesn't accept me.

Yes, I've repented—repeatedly—but God knows.

And, I know, and I'm hiding my sins so that (hopefully) no one else learns about them.

I'm trying to get rid of them before others find out.

What would they think about me?

I don't like myself. Actually, I hate myself.

How could anyone else like me if they only knew?

How can God like me, let alone love me?

If He only knew.

Oh, I forgot He already knows.

He knows everything.

Have you ever been there? Under the massive weight of *GUILT.*

Most, if not ALL of us, have.

Not knowing how to get out of the vicious cycle. We screw up—we try to hide it—we try to justify it; but no matter what, we feel all the guilt of the world on us. Finally, we repent (again and again and again). We tell God we won't do it again—we promise we won't do it again—we ask Him to help us. Then some time (maybe a short time) later we do it all over again. We repeat the cycle. And the *god* of this world laughs—"rinse and repeat", "rinse and repeat", "rinse and repeat", "rinse and repeat".

Then we ask, "How come the Holy Spirit didn't help us?"

We cried.

We repented.

We tried.

We promised.

Why?

Probably, because we're just one of the irredeemable. Right?

Not like the rest of God's children who never (or hardly ever) have these problems. They must be able to walk in righteousness—because I don't see them having the same horrible problems I do. That just proves I am irredeemable.

It's about enough to want to make you quit. RIGHT?

Oh, how the devil enjoys making us feel crazy—out of control. And, what he doesn't invoke directly, he's well-trained us to do his job for him. Oh, how he laughs.

The weight of *GUILT* can make us miss our intimate relationship with God. But it's time to learn something here and now. If you've repented, it's not the sins that are messing up your relationship with God, it's the *GUILT.* And, if we knew everyone else's secrets, we'd find they're in the same struggle.

Am I saying, keep living under SIN?

NO.

Then what?

Do you remember chapter two and chapter twelve in the first book?

Where we discussed, we cannot do anything to be worthy or good enough to reach God or stay in His Presence.

First, it's by His Grace alone.

"For by **Grace** you have been **saved** through **Faith**; and that not of yourselves, it is the gift of God; **not** as a **result** of (any) **works**, so that no one may boast." (Ephesians 2:8–9)

Second, our righteousness, on our very best day, is like filthy rags.

"For we have all become like one who is unclean [ceremonially, like a leper], and **ALL** our **righteousness** (our best deeds of rightness and justice) are like **filthy rags** or a **polluted garment**." (Isaiah 64:6)

And, third, at our very best, we're unworthy servants.

"Even so on your part, when you have done everything that was assigned and commanded you, say, we are **unworthy servants** [possessing no merit, for we have not gone beyond our obligation]; we have [merely] done what was our duty to do." (Luke 17:10)

And the manual continues with, "A Word to the Wise."

Don't be religious. Don't fake out yourself, others, or God. Be real. Be honest. Love the Truth. We can never be perfect enough. We can never be good enough. God's Grace saved us, not our righteousness or any efforts of our own; at best, we're unworthy servants. Our only recourse is to exercise the powers of *CHOICE* and *YIELDING*, which are the *ONLY* powers given to us.

Do you remember the secret you learned in the manual? *"We're a vessel to whomever we yield."* Since you can never be good enough on your own—stop trying—start yielding.

So how do we get out from under the vicious cycle of SIN and GUILT?

Yielding to the Lord.

So how does that work in practicality?

First, we need to recognize the maze the *god* of this world has us in—*SIN*—then *GUILT;* more *SIN;* more *GUILT*—an endless cycle.

Second, we need to accept what God has told us: We were saved by Grace, not by (any) works we can do. That our righteousness (on our very best day(s)) is like filthy rags. And at best, we're unworthy servants.

Third, we need to accept that God loves us no matter what. That's not "sloppy grace." That's not justifying we continue in sins without repentance.

Forth, when we repent, it's accepting we don't mean for the sins to cause *SIN* (separating us from God).

Fifth, we need to stop listening to the enemy, others, and especially ourselves, about how we deserve no more chances with His Grace. Remember, we can *NEVER* be good enough.

Sixth, therefore, understanding these things, we **YIELD** ourselves to Him and allow His Spirit to flow from our innermost beings and allow His Grace to cleanse us. This time. The next time. And the many times after. For as long as we're human and on this earth. Remember, it's called **Sanctification**. The ever present—ever lasting process that will continue until the day we go home to see Him.

Seventh, we will then find the Peace of God will flow through our hearts and minds and we can walk in *True Faith* [as we talked about in the first manual]. Not disregarding *SIN*—but now having a new way in which to walk through it. A walk where God walks with us and we walk with him—humbly—in Truth; no lies; not fooling ourselves; not trying to fool others; no longer hiding from anyone—especially ourselves.

Understanding even more how gracious He is to look through the lens of Jesus' blood to see us forgiven of all sins—that blood and the seal of the promised Holy Spirit in us is our *true HOPE*.

Guaranteed: If we don't get out from under this guilt, then we're held and will remain captive.

UNDER JUDGEMENTS

Remember our previous discussion about judgements. How God tells us not to judge ['krinō'] others' characters.

Well, I have bad news—we've been set up for failure. The *god* of this world wants us living, judging others—not the right kinds of judgement, as discussed. But by 'krinō'ing them with God's white throne judgement—judging their characters.

It's all around us. It's in the people we live and associate with. It's in the people we work with. It's at the grocery store. It's in our churches. It's in the TV shows we watch. And more.

Why?

Because as we fall to these temptations throughout our daily lives, just as he trained us to run the maze, then he can make us miss out on the intimate relationship with God that's there waiting for us.

Guaranteed: If we don't get out from under these judgements, then we're held and will remain captive.

UNDER CURSES, ANGER, HATE, AND UNFORGIVENESS

These, too, are the same. As described in much detail in the manual, God's people have been set up for failure in these areas as well. Again, as we fall for and carry out these mistakes, as the enemy has trained us to run the maze, he can make us miss out on the intimate relationship with God there waiting for us.

Guaranteed: If we don't get out from under curses, anger, hate, and unforgiveness, then we're held and will remain captive.

UNDER DECEPTIONS

We discussed deceptions in the first book, so I won't reiterate them here.

The *god* of this world has built his maze of deceptions and interwove them into our minds. Our old nature is his sandbox where he keeps us playing, building sandcastles and sand creations that go nowhere. And definitely not into the Presence of God.

So, to keep us in any of those deceptions can make us miss out on the intimate relationship with God waiting for us.

Guaranteed: If we don't get out from under these deceptions, then we're held and will remain captive.

OBVIOUSLY, PHYSICAL CAPTIVITY OR ENSLAVEMENTS

It happened to Israel many times. They lived as slaves in captivity, serving their task masters until a time when God would set them free. To only go into captivity again and again for the stubbornness of their hearts. Until Israel could learn the lessons God wanted them to learn.

We would all agree that it's beyond tragic when abductors take someone captive or enslave them physically—and we know that many people around the world have experienced this and continue to experience it today. Taken as work slaves. Taken as sex slaves. Devastatingly horrible! I can only imagine, and you also, unless it's happened to you personally.

While this subject is obvious and beyond horrifying, with no words to describe the atrocities, most do *NOT* realize the *Captivity* of the heart and mind are *MUCH WORSE.*

These people know they are slaves and held in captivity. Begging, pleading, praying to get out.

WE DO NOT.

CHAPTER FIVE

EGYPT IN THE CHURCH

SET GOD'S PEOPLE FREE

M OSES TOLD PHARAOH, "LET My people go."

In Exodus 7:14-18,

"Then the LORD said to Moses, 'Pharaoh's heart is stubborn; he refuses to let the people go.

Go to Pharaoh in the morning as he is going out to the water, and station yourself to meet him on the bank of the Nile; and you shall take in your hand the staff that was turned into a serpent.

You shall say to him, "The LORD, the God of the Hebrews, sent me to you, saying, 'Let My people go, that they may serve Me in the wilderness. But behold, you have not listened until now.'

Thus says the LORD, 'By this you shall know that I am the LORD: behold, I will strike the water that is in the Nile with the staff that is in my hand, and it will be turned to blood.

The fish that are in the Nile will die, and the Nile will become foul, and the

Egyptians will find difficulty in drinking water from the Nile.'"'"

But the heart of Pharaoh was hardened, and he did not let the people go on Moses' words, so God sent nine more plagues.

Continuing on in Exodus 8:1 through Exodus 12:41, came the remaining plagues.

Next came the Plague of Frogs—but Pharaoh would not let the people of Israel go.

Then came the Plague of Gnats—but Pharaoh would not let the people of Israel go.

Then came the Plague of Insects—but Pharaoh would not let the people of Israel go.

Then came the Plague of Pestilence—but Pharaoh would not let the people of Israel go.

Then came the Plague of Boils—but Pharaoh would not let the people of Israel go.

Then came the Plague of Hail—but Pharaoh would not let the people of Israel go.

Then came the Plague of Locusts—but Pharaoh would not let the people of Israel go.

Then came Darkness over the Land—but Pharaoh would not let the people of Israel go.

Finally came the Plague of Passover—where the Lord killed all the firstborn in Egypt, but passed over all in Israel who had followed Moses's instructions.

Then, and only then, did Pharaoh let the people of Israel go.

INTO THE WILDERNESS FOR FORTY YEARS

When finally freed, the Israelites were *NOT* ready to proceed to the promised land. Instead, they needed to go into the wilderness for forty years.

Why?

Because God needed to purge them of their old ways of thinking as slaves who, by *Stockholm Syndrome,* learned to feel "safe" inside that captivity.

You'd think that should be easy—to shrug off slavery and captivity. Right?

I mean, after being slaves—waiting, begging, and praying to God to be freed for over four hundred years—you'd think that should be enough all by itself and they'd jump at the chance to be free. Right?

Like they would want freedom more than anything—want it like *NOTHING* else—do *ANYTHING* to keep it; especially with the certain reward of getting to go to the promised land. A land of "milk and honey." Right?

The problem was the deeply engrained "safe" feeling they'd gained inside of captivity.

So, what did Israel do?

"On the fifteenth day of the second month after their departure from the land of Egypt. The whole congregation of the sons of Israel grumbled against Moses and Aaron in the wilderness. The sons of Israel said to them, 'Would that we had died by the Lord's hand in the land of Egypt, when we sat by the pots of meat, when we ate bread to the full; for you have brought us out into this wilderness to kill this whole assembly with hunger.'" (Exodus 16:1-3)

Forget the land of "milk and honey".

71

"We sat by pots of meat."

"We ate bread to the full."

"We know our 'comfort' and our 'safe' zone."

"Send us back!"

This was how the next forty years were to be.

So what happened in those forty years?

Well, if each generation is about twenty years long, then forty years is two generations. And two generations' worth of captive ideas needed to die with those generations. Allowing new generations, free of those encumbrances, to move forward.

THE PURGING

This forty years of purging was to set Israel free from all the things that *BOUND* them—to teach them to trust the God of Israel again—to learn that only He can provide them "fresh manna from Heaven", each and every day.

In the same way, God sends us into the wilderness for our "forty years", whether figurative or literal, to purge us. To set us free. From all that *BINDS* us—from our many "captive" years.

*And, like it or not, **WE NEED IT**.*

NO other option is available to us. As was for Israel. So, kick against the pricks and cry to go back, all you want. But get ready for God to say, *"NO."*

HE LOVES US TOO MUCH!

In Matthew 6:9-13 in the Lord's Prayer, Jesus said,

"Pray, then, in this way:

'Our Father who is in Heaven, hallowed be Your name. Your kingdom come. Your will be done. On earth as it is in Heaven.

Give us this day our daily bread. And forgive us our debts, as we also have forgiven our debtors.

And do not lead us into temptation, but deliver us from evil. [For Yours is the kingdom and the power and the glory forever. Amen.]'"

Jesus only had to go into the wilderness for forty days to fast and pray, but He understood God would provide *"our daily bread"* for all the days (and years) that we will need to go through our wildernesses.

He understood one thing more about that manna from God.

In Matthew 4:1-4 we're told,

"Then Jesus was led up by the Spirit into the wilderness to be tempted by the devil. And after He had fasted forty days and forty nights, He then became hungry.

And the tempter came and said to Him, 'If You are the Son of God, command that these stones become bread.'

But He answered and said, 'It is written, man shall not live on bread alone, but on **EVERY WORD** that proceeds out of the **MOUTH** of **GOD**.'"

So better than *"our daily bread"* is **EVERY WORD** that proceeds out of the **MOUTH** of **GOD**.

Can we learn that secret?

Can we get a hold of that truth?

We need to!

THE WARNING

As mentioned previously, when the children of Israel had to endure the hardships of the wilderness, many, many times they wanted to go back to their old slavery in Egypt. When they finally realized they were stuck out there, they did not accept it willingly.

Instead, they decided if they couldn't go back to the "comforts" and "safety" of Egypt they would bring those "comforts" and "safety" to their time stuck in the wilderness.

So what did they do?

They made themselves "new gods" made of gold and silver in the same fashion they'd learned in their *Stockholm* times in Egypt.

In Exodus 32:1-7, we see Israel made themselves "a Golden Calf", as well as got their current leader (Aaron) to commission it,

"Now when the people saw that Moses delayed to come down from the mountain, the people assembled about Aaron and said to him, 'Come, make us a *god* who will go before us; as for this Moses, the man who brought us up from the land of Egypt, we do not know what has become of him.'

Aaron said to them, 'Tear off the gold rings which are in the ears of your wives, your sons, and your daughters, and bring them to me.'

Then all the people tore off the gold rings which were in their ears and brought them to Aaron. He took this from their hand and fashioned it with a graving tool and made it into a molten calf; and they said, 'This is your god, O Israel, who brought you up from the land of Egypt.'

Now when Aaron saw this, he built an altar before it; and Aaron made a proclamation and said, 'Tomorrow shall be a feast to the "lord".' So the next day they rose early and offered burnt offerings, and brought peace offerings; and the people sat down to eat and to drink, and rose up to play."

HOW SAD!

How sad. It was surprisingly easy for the *ex-Stockholm-captives* to revert to their old ways.

How sad. That they could get their new leader(s) out in the wilderness with them to agree to create *NEW false gods*—a *NEW "lord"* "who brought you out of Egypt". *NEW false Belief Systems*—completely based on their *OLD false Belief Systems*.

How sad. That we will do *EXACTLY* the same thing—in our times in the wilderness. Without intervention, we *ALL* will build *NEW false gods* and *NEW false Belief Systems*. Based on the *OLD false Belief Systems* we endured and should've been free from. If we had let the wilderness do its intended purpose.

Then continuing in Exodus 32:7-10,

"Then the Lord spoke to Moses, 'Go down at once, for your people, whom you brought up from the land of Egypt, have corrupted themselves. They have quickly turned aside from the way which I commanded them.

They have made for themselves a molten calf, and have worshiped it and have sacrificed to it and said, "This is your *god*, O Israel, who brought you up from the land of Egypt!"'

The LORD said to Moses, 'I have seen this people, and behold, they are an obstinate people. Now then let Me alone, that My anger may burn against them and that I may destroy them; and I will make of you a great nation.'"

We need to note that Israel did this *AFTER* witnessing miracle *AFTER* miracle *AFTER* miracle from God—from the plagues that freed them from Egypt, to the parting of the Red Sea, to drowning of the Egyptian army following them, to daily manna for forty years.

But we wouldn't do that. Would we?

Unfortunately, YES!

Considering God's response to Israel and our potential to create "new gods" during our trials in the wilderness, let us be warned never to allow ourselves or others to manipulate us in this way.

Our wilderness times are meant to purge us of all those things that held us captive. So, set your mind and face like granite to allow God to do that *FULL* process in you. Otherwise, you might end up worse off than when you began.

Not a good choice!

WILDERNESS BOTTOM LINE

LAYERS AND LAYERS OF THE ONION, AGAIN

As mentioned previously, *Belief Systems* and our *Stockholm indoctrinations* have many, many layers. Over many years and experiences, they were built, layer upon layer, like an onion.

Therefore, just as it took many years to build them, it may very well take many years to undo them.

A TIME OF PURIFICATION

In case you haven't figured it out by now, the wilderness is a ***time*** of ***Purification***—and that ***time*** and its ***length*** is up to **God**—who loves us; and knows how long and what it will take to purge those captivities from us.

Do you understand you have a choice?

ARE YOU WILLING TO PAY THE PRICE?

You can choose to stay in Egypt in bondage, captive in *false Belief Systems*, or you can **choose** to **pay** the **price** and go into God's wilderness [for you] for the time needed. God's timing for you might be short—it might be long.

ARE ALL WILDERNESSES THE SAME?

NO.

God's wilderness for you may differ from what He needs to do in me—and vice versa. This will be true for all of us. He's in control and will oversee each of our wildernesses, in the same way He has every hair numbered on our heads.

"Are not five sparrows sold for two pennies? And [yet] **not one** of them is **forgotten** or **uncared** for in the **Presence** of **God**.

But [even] the very hairs of your head are all numbered. Do not be struck with fear or seized with alarm; you are of greater worth than many [flocks] of sparrows." (Luke 12:6-7)

If He oversees and cares for each hair on our heads—actually having numbered each hair—so He knows when a hair is combed or falls out; then He certainly can be trusted to oversee our lives; whether or not in the wilderness.

Some will call their wildernesses "trials and tribulations." Some will call them "going to hell and back." It doesn't matter what you call it—it'll be God's time to purge you. Accept it as His time of Grace to you.

Understand, He will provide a way out. And in the end, it will be worth it.

I can guarantee as a forty-year survivor that they are NOT fun.

Even if they are short.

Now I'm not sure that I was in a single wilderness for all of those forty years, but if not, I was in and out of a bunch of wildernesses during that stretch. No matter what it was, it was what I needed, as prescribed by our loving Father.

For me, I guess it took forty years to "kill off" two generations' worth of crap out of my life. Removing *"bad thinking"*, *"bad thought processes"*, *"bad Belief Systems"*, as well as a lot of *pride* and *ego*.

Maybe, if you can hear the call from the Father through this work:

> *listen sooner,*
>
> *listen better,*
>
> *humble yourself more,*

then you can get through it in less time than I did.

I really hope so for you!

What I can promise is, no matter what, it will be worth it.

IF you don't go back to Egypt—even in your mind—**OR** create "new gods" based on your old *Stockholm* captive *Belief Systems*.

Therefore, choose your time in the wilderness—as a good thing and a needed time in your life!

Note: When we hear God's call to the wilderness, as is His call to anything for any change or season in our lives, there's a ***special dispensation*** of ***His Spirit*** for us if we listen and obey in that call and time.

This is one thing I've learned and can attest to, that in over fifty-plus years of the Lord walking with me (even when I wasn't walking with Him)—when He by His Spirit calls to us in these times of change for our lives—if we respond positively to Him; He will give us a ***special dispensation*** of ***His Grace*** to walk through them.

Let me assure you that this dispensation of Grace is a beautiful thing.

It's "worth its weight in gold" to see us through.

GOD'S CALL TO THE CHURCH

*God is calling to **ALL** of His people to come out of Egypt.*

Then, to go into the wilderness to find Him (again).

And, just as Moses cried out, so God is calling to **ALL** the leaders holding God's people "captive" and "stuck in bondage" in the churches:

"LET MY PEOPLE GO!"

"SET MY PEOPLE FREE!"

CHAPTER SIX

GOD GAVE THEM TASKMASTERS

ISRAEL'S FREEDOM WAS SHORT-LIVED

F OLLOWING THEIR LIBERATION AND forty years in the wilderness,
many Israelites continued to reject a personal relationship with God
and instead demanded new leaders—new rulers—new taskmasters; to
enslave them once more.

The idea of setting God's people free was ***NOT*** to go from ***one bondage***
into the ***next captivity***.

Yet, since the people of Israel would not govern themselves, God gave them
Judges, then Prophets, then Kings (Acts 13:17-23)—then back to slavery
again under foreign nations, foreign kings, and foreign *gods*. And even
when they finally returned to Israel, priests and tyrannical rulers like the
Pharisees and Sadducees subjected them, imposing the law without the
Spirit of God.

ALL BECAUSE ISRAEL WOULD NOT LISTEN TO GOD, THE FATHER

All because they chose to not *KNOW* Him—to have an intimate personal relationship with Him [see the first book for clarity on this subject]. The one and only, the True and Living God who created the universe, who gives us life. So, He gave them task masters again and again and again—because of the stubbornness of their hearts.

WE DO THE SAME

Many times, we don't listen or want to learn from our times in our wildernesses—because of the stubbornness of our hearts—so God allows us to have many task masters to rule over our lives.

SUCH AS MEN'S "AUTHORITY" RULING IN THE CHURCHES

But you say, aren't we supposed to submit to men's [or women's] authority in the church?

*YES, and **NO**.*

The **YES**: God gave us leaders, especially when we were young Believers, to protect us, shepherd us, and oversee us in our early years of growth.

As seen in First Peter 5:5,

"Likewise, you who are ***younger*** and of lesser rank, be ***subject*** to the ***elders*** (the ministers and spiritual guides of the church) — [giving them due respect and yielding to their counsel]. Clothe (apron) yourselves, all of you, with humility [as the garb of a servant, so that its covering cannot possibly be stripped from you, with freedom from pride and arrogance] toward one another. For God sets Himself against the proud (the insolent, the overbearing, the disdainful, the presumptuous, the boastful) — [and He opposes, frustrates, and defeats them], but gives grace (favor, blessing) to the humble."

THE WRONG TASK MASTERS

The *NO:* In Ezekiel 34:1-4, Ezekiel prophecies against the Shepherds of Israel,

"Then the word of the LORD came to me saying,

Son of man, *prophesy* against the *shepherds* of *Israel*. Prophesy and say to those shepherds, 'Thus says the Lord GOD, "Woe, shepherds of Israel who have been feeding themselves! Should not the shepherds feed the flock?

You eat the fat and clothe yourselves with the wool; you slaughter the fat sheep without feeding the flock.

Those who are sickly you have not strengthened, the diseased you have not healed, the broken you have not bound up, the scattered you have not brought back, nor have you sought for the lost; but with *force* and with *severity* you have *dominated* them.""""

The same verses in the AMP read:

"And the word of the Lord came to me, saying,

Son of man, *prophesy* against the *shepherds* of *Israel;* prophesy and say to them, even to the *[spiritual] shepherds*, 'Thus says the Lord God: *"Woe* to the *[spiritual] shepherds* of *Israel* who feed themselves! Should not the shepherds feed the sheep?

You eat the fat; you clothe yourselves with the wool; you kill the fatlings, but you do not feed the sheep.

The *diseased* and **weak** you have not **strengthened**, the **sick** you have not **healed**, the **hurt** and **crippled** you have not **bandaged**, those *gone astray* you have not **brought back**, the **lost** you have not **sought** to *find*, but with *force* and **hardhearted harshness** you have **ruled** them.""

The word *force* in the Hebrew is 'chozqah' (khoz-KAH) which means *"strength," "force," "violence," "severely,"* and *"vigorously [taken]"* from the root words 'chozeq' (kho'-zek) meaning *"strength," "power,"* and *"powerful"* and 'chazaq' (khaw-zak') meaning *"to be or grow firm or strong," "became mighty," "became powerful," "became strong," "been arrogant," "gain ascendancy," "making himself strong,"* and *"seized [power]."*

The word *severity* or **hardhearted harshness** in the Hebrew is 'perek' (peh'-rek) which means *"[done in] harshness," "[done with] severity,"* and *"[done] rigorously."*

The word *dominated* or **ruled** in the Hebrew is 'radah' (rah-DAH) which means *"to have dominion [over]," "rule [over]," "dominate [over]," "dominated [over],"* and *"subdues or subdued [those below them]."*

So the words "with *force* and *severity* [hardhearted harshness] you have **dominated** [ruled] them,"

In the Hebrew, could be expanded to read:

"Being **arrogant** they **seized** and became **mighty**, gained **ascendancy**, took **power** by **force**; they did it **rigorously**, with **severity** and **harshness** by **subduing** those below them, **creating** an **atmosphere** where they can **rule** and have **dominion over** them."

Can you see the **ARROGANCE** of those [spiritual] shepherds?

Does it remind you of Lucifer's arrogance, the *god* of this world, and why God expelled him from Heaven?

They are one and the same.

Leaders trained by their demon rulers over them.

First Peter 5, verses one through three, admonishes those leaders.

"I **warn** and **counsel** the **elders** among you (the **pastors** and **spiritual guides** of the church) as a fellow elder and as an eyewitness [called to testify] of the sufferings of Christ, as well as a sharer in the glory (the honor and splendor) that is to be revealed (disclosed, unfolded):

Tend (nurture, guard, guide, and fold) the **flock** of **God** that is [your **responsibility**], not by coercion or constraint, but willingly; not dishonorably motivated by the advantages and profits [belonging to the office], but eagerly and cheerfully;

Not domineering [as arrogant, dictatorial, and overbearing persons] over those in your charge, but being **examples** (patterns and models of Christian living) to the flock (the congregation)."

Furthermore, in Second Corinthians 1:24, we read,

"**Not** that we **lord** it **over** your **faith**, but are (co) workers **with** you for your **joy**; for in your **faith** you are standing firm."

The word **faith** in the Greek is 'pistis' (PIS-tis) which means, *"faith," "faithfulness," "pledge,"* and *"proof"*; which comes from the root word 'peithō' (pay'-tho) which means *"to persuade," "to have confidence," "listen," "obeying,"* and *"trusting."*

These leaders are being warned to *NEVER* lord (dominate) over the listening, hearing, obedience, trust, and faith with God of the Believers under their care.

THOSE WHO FAIL THESE WARNINGS

Are the type of leaders that control their people with *Stockholm-type false Belief Systems.* They are *NOT* leaders operating **IN Christ** *[in the Anointing]*; they are leaders under the rule of demons operating out of false Christs [false anointings] the spirit of the antichrist—see the first book.

These leaders, men or women, are "Tyrannical Ideologues" in the church world, in the same way Mark Levin [TV personality, author, political commentator] designates this term for "off the spectrum", arrogant, dictatorial people in the political world. These folks relentlessly force their ideologies on everyone as the *ONLY Truth;* and they as the *ONLY purveyors* and *source* of that *Truth.*

WHAT GOD REQUIRES OF THEM

All builders and leaders need to understand clearly what God is requiring of them.

As we are told in First Corinthians 3:11-17,

"For no other foundation can anyone lay than that which is [already] laid, which is Jesus ***Christ (the Anointing).***

But if anyone builds upon the Foundation, whether it be with gold, silver, precious stones, wood, hay, straw,

The work of each [one] will become [plainly, openly] known (shown for what it is); for the day [of ***Christ (the Anointing)***] will disclose and declare it, because it will be revealed with fire, and the fire will test and critically appraise the character and worth of the work each person has done.

If the work which any person has built on this Foundation [any ***product*** of his ***efforts*** whatever] survives [this test], he will get his reward.

But if any person's work is burned up [under the test], he will ***suffer*** the ***loss*** [of it all, losing his reward], though he himself will be saved, but only as [one who has passed] through fire. [Job 23:10]

Do you not discern and understand that [each one of] ***you*** are ***God's*** *temple (His sanctuary),* and that *God's Spirit* has *His permanent dwelling* in *you* [to be at home in you, collectively as a church and also individually]?

If anyone does *HURT* to *God's temple* or *CORRUPTS* it [with *false doctrines*] or *DESTROYS* it, *God* will *DO HURT* to him and bring him to the *CORRUPTION* of *DEATH* and *DESTROY* him. For the *temple* of *God* is *Holy* (sacred to Him) and that [temple] you [the believing church and its individual believers] are."

YET SOME WILL ARGUE

But we're not responsible for these failings—it was the originators of these packs made with demon spirit rulers (creating "denominations") in the churches—not us. We're victims as well. We grew up this way in the church and were ignorant of other options. And as *Stockholm survivors,* we unknowingly became perpetrators, generations later. Shouldn't we receive extra grace for this?

NO.

God will hold each person accountable for how they listened to Him and behaved in His Church.

THIS IS THE WARNING TO ALL BUILDERS AND LEADERS

You need to reevaluate your positions and responsibilities over God's flock in view of the [disinfecting Son] Light, as revealed by the Spirit of God. You must clearly understand what God will require of you, holding you into account.

It would be better for you to STOP, for now, and not *HURT God's temple* [*people*] nor *CORRUPT* it [with *false doctrines*] nor *DESTROY* it, then to build falsely and be called into account. In the same mind, it would be better for you to allow the Spirit of God to complete this work in you before returning to any such position, if He so allows.

THE TRANSITION

Continuing on from Ezekiel 34 previously, in verses 7-12, 16 and 23 we see,

"Therefore, you *[spiritual] shepherds,* hear the word of the LORD:

'As I live,' declares the Lord GOD, 'surely because My flock has become a prey, My flock has even become food for all the beasts of the field for lack of a shepherd, and My shepherds did not search for My flock, but rather the shepherds fed themselves and did not feed My flock;'

Therefore, you *[spiritual] shepherds,* hear the word of the LORD:

'Thus says the Lord GOD, "Behold, I am against the *[spiritual] shepherds,* and I will demand My sheep from them and make them cease from feeding sheep. So the shepherds will not feed themselves anymore, but I *will deliver My flock* from *their mouth,* so that they will not be food for them."

For thus says the Lord GOD, "Behold, I Myself *will search* for *My sheep* and seek them out.

As a shepherd cares for his herd in the day when he is among his scattered sheep, so I will care for My sheep and *will deliver* them from *all* the *places* to which they were scattered on a cloudy and gloomy day.

I *will seek* the *lost,* bring back the *scattered, bind up* the *broken* and *strengthen* the *sick;* but the fat and the strong I will destroy. I will feed them with judgment.

Then I will set over them *ONE Shepherd,* My *Servant David,* and He will feed them; He *will feed* them *Himself* and be *their shepherd.*"'"

It's obvious that God doesn't like or want the wrong *[spiritual] shepherds, leaders,* or *Task Masters* over His people. And He will gather His people from all the places they were scattered. He will seek them out; bring them back; bind up the brokenhearted; and strengthen the sick. Then He says He will put **ONE Shepherd**, My **Servant David**, over them to keep them safe and bring them back to health.

Since Ezekiel lived hundreds of years after King David, do you think God got it wrong talking about His Servant David?

I'm going to go with NO.

God didn't make a mistake here.

Who was the *Promised One* from the line of David? *Jesus.*

So what does that mean?

It means that *ALL* of God's sheep [us] are to be under **ONE Shepherd**, My **Servant** [from the line of] David, **Jesus Himself.**

THE RIGHT LEADERS THAT GOD WANTS

In Ephesians 4:11–16 it states,

"And, He gave some as apostles, and some as prophets, and some as evangelists, and some as pastors and teachers,

For the **EQUIPPING** of the Saints, for the work of service,

To the **BUILDING UP**, of the Body of Christ;

UNTIL, we all attain to the unity of the faith.

And, of the knowledge of the Son of God, to a **mature man**, to the measure of the stature which belongs to the **Fullness** of **Christ** [the

Anointing].

From whom the ***whole Body***, being ***fitted*** and ***held together***, by what ***EVERY JOINT SUPPLIES***,

According to the ***PROPER WORKING*** of ***EACH INDIVIDUAL PART***."

So, what does that mean?

It means that the Lord has tasked ***ALL*** these leaders to do three things:

First, ***EQUIP*** the Saints.

Second, ***BUILD UP*** the Body of Christ.

And third, ***UNTIL***—yes, ***UNTIL***, not forever, only, ***UNTIL—UNTIL*** we attain to the unity of the faith.

When we attain that teaching, training, and infusion of ***CHRIST*** *(the ANOINTING)*, we're to be released to do the jobs and whatever functions the Lord would have us do.

As explained in the first book, the people (the peons), the sheep, the Believers, and the Saints are the ones at the top who are supposed to do the work. We received the task of carrying *the **Anointing*** into the world through our everyday lives.

So, contrary to the Western world's leadership interpretations, the leaders have a ***Limited Responsibility*** for a ***Limited Time*** to do as the Father wants. Yes, in the beginning and along the path, their job is to oversee and help protect the sheep; but more importantly, they're to undergird the people and raise them up, building up the Body of Christ.

THE RIGHT RELATIONSHIP

These leaders, to the exact opposite of lording it over our faith, are supposed to be ***coequal workers*** for our joy and the building up our ***faith*** ['pistis' (PIS-tis)]—which is our pledge, our proof, our persuasion, our confidence, our ability to listen, obey, and trust God the Father and Jesus, as the Head of the Body of Christ.

When we are spiritually young, **YES**, we should submit to the (hopefully good) leaders, elders, pastors, teachers, prophets, and apostles whom the Father has commissioned to oversee and raise us into maturity.

But then later, **NO**. Our destiny was never to remain as children under authoritarians forever. We're actually supposed to grow up and become coequal workers in the Body of Christ.

"Be *subject [submit]* to one another out of reverence for *Christ [the Anointing]*."(Ephesians 5:21)

The word *subject* or *submit* in the Greek is 'hupotassō' (hoop-ot-as'-so), which means *"to place or rank under," "to subject," "to obey," "put in subjection," "subjected," "subjecting," "submissive," "submit."* Which is from the prime root 'hupo' (hoo-PO), which means *"by," "under," "about," "hands," "under: power."*

So, a simple view of subjection or submission from the Greek means "to put the hand inside or under [the glove]." Therefore, we are now to be *subject* to *one another* placing ourselves under one another as coequal servants and workers in the Body of Christ.

Looking back at Authority (as taught in the first book), we determined we must put ourselves inside or under God's Authority to have Authority. From this same place under God's Authority, we can then choose to put ourselves in subjection to one another as coequal workers in Christ.

At which point, *ALL* of God's sheep [us] can be under **ONE Shepherd, My Servant** [from the line of] **David**.

LET'S LOOK AT JESUS, OUR EXAMPLE

Yes, even Jesus was raised and taught in the temple until twelve years old.

But did that continue?

In Luke 2:41-47 we see,

"Now [Jesus's] parents went to Jerusalem every year at the Feast of the Passover. And when He became twelve, they went up there according to the custom of the Feast;

And as they were returning, after spending the full number of days, the boy Jesus stayed behind in Jerusalem. But His parents were unaware of it, but supposed Him to be in the caravan, and went a day's journey; and they began looking for Him among their relatives and acquaintances.

When they did not find Him, they returned to Jerusalem looking for Him. Then, after three days, they found Him in the temple, sitting in the midst of the teachers, both *listening* to them and *asking* them questions. And *ALL* who heard Him were amazed at *His understanding* and *His answers.*"

We never see that tutelage in the temple continue anywhere in the Gospels. Jesus had grown up and had become their equal—instead of remaining a student forever, and to the contrary, at twelve, He began teaching the elders in the temple.

Why?

Because He'd matured—grown up in the Spirit and no longer needed that submissive place of teaching and protection. Jesus was now a man.

In Jewish culture, when a young person reaches the age of twelve, they are bar mitzvah'd (for boys) or bat mitzvah'd (for girls)—a rite of passage signifying adulthood.

God never said to the Jews, nor the Church, "Stay babies forever." Yet we have a culture in the churches nowadays (and true for a long time) that we are to stay babies (little children) under the strict rulership of the "leaders". Until those leaders decide, it's time to permit us to gradually advance within their *Belief Systems* to the levels, positions, functions, and leadership roles they've designated for us.

UNTIL, AND ONLY, UNTIL

Paul instructed us that this is only *"UNTIL,* we all attain to the unity of the faith." Therefore, it's clear and well understood that *ALL* the leaders' jobs are an *"UNTIL ministry."*

Unfortunately, some (maybe many) of the leaders, still wanting to retain power, will argue that "attaining to the unity of the faith" is a lifetime process. Therefore, their job (and power and control) will *NEVER* be done.

FALSE.

Paul continues in Galatians 4:1-2,

"Now what I mean is that as long as the inheritor (heir) is a child and under age, he does not differ from a slave (or a bond servant), although he is the master of all the estate;

But he is under guardians and administrators or trustees *UNTIL* the date fixed by his Father."

All of us, as sons and daughters, are heirs in *Christ*. And while "under age" we are to remain "under guardians and administrators or trustees". But note: There's an end. It's for a limited time while we're underage. And only *UNTIL* the date or time set by the Father.

As explained in the first book: Leaders must position themselves at, the bottom of the bottom, to support the Saints, to lift (build) them up, and do *EVERYTHING* possible to *WORK THEMSELVES OUT OF A JOB.* Then they're functioning *IN CHRIST.* If not, they're *ALL* operating under *false Christs* and *false anointings,* making them *false apostles, false prophets,* and *false leaders.*

BUT ISN'T THIS THE NORM?

Haven't we done it this way "forever?"

Who am I to question this deeply engrained and well-accepted *"sacred cow"* practice [of leadership dominance] in the churches?

Actually, I'm nobody special. Just a plain 'ol Believer who wants God, His word, and the Truth to prevail.

REMEMBER "DENOMINATIONS" ARE "DEMONS-IN-NATIONS"

Demon rulers that rule over all these denominations, non-denominations, and *false Belief Systems.* They love this stuff—they really get off on it. Think about it. The devil fell for the love of ego, pride, and power—and the leaders under him love the same. Of course, they'd cloak it under false spirituality and fake religiously.

To all the leaders who will decry blasphemy, heretic, or heresy at this point [if they haven't already]—for revealing their secrets—for dare touching their *"sacred cow"* and *"golden calf"* of leadership dominance over the sheep; I pray you humble yourselves, repent, and return to the Lord, His simple Truth, and His love from where you began. I will deal with a lot more on this subject later, so hang on to your seats.

FOR ALL WHO SAY, "WHAT'S HE TALKING ABOUT HERE?"

We *ALL* know that these functions are the reason leaders were appointed—and as sheep, we are to continue following the shepherds—until they instruct otherwise.

Right?

WRONG.

How many leaders ruled over Adam and Eve?

How about Enoch?

How about Abraham?

How about Israel, the man?

How about King David?

How about Soloman?

How about Ezekiel?

How about Isaiah?

How about all the other prophets?

How about John the Baptist?

How about Jesus?

Yes, we established Jesus was in the temple until twelve. He did that out of obedience to his earthly and heavenly Fathers. But we *NEVER* see Him under that authority again.

The simple point I'm making is there's a right time to be under men's teaching and authority—but then there's the time that we're supposed to have matured, grown up, and now be operating in and out of the Presence of God—by the Spirit; fully refined; under the leadership of the **ONE Shepherd, Jesus.** Operating in a coequal functioning relationship to **ALL** the members of the Body of Christ.

Remember, in Philippians 3 above,

"So let those [of us] who are **spiritually mature** and **full-grown** have this mind and hold these convictions; and if in any respect you have a different attitude of mind, God will make that clear to you also."

And in Luke 6:40,

"A pupil [disciple] is not superior to his teacher, but **everyone** [when he is] **completely trained** (readjusted, restored, set to rights, and perfected) will be **LIKE** his teacher."

God wants His people to grow up as mature sons and daughters. Walking with Him. Seeing what He's doing—hearing what He's saying—then doing and saying the same.

Oops!

Blasphemy again?

Nope.

But won't we all go "crazy" or lose our minds if we don't just follow the leaders, as we've always been taught?

Nope.

But won't there be some (or a lot) who will go off the rails—thinking they "hear from God the best" and no one can correct them?

Sure, some will.

But that's the chance we take in following God and walking in the Spirit. Unfortunately, those same ones would've probably done the same thing anyway—with or without constraints.

Of course, there are precautions. I covered them in the first book. As well as I will continue to cover them more as we progress through this book. So, if we learn to walk *HUMBLY* with our God; if we learn to walk by and in His Spirit; if we allow the Father to *WORK* His *WORK* in us that we truly *BELIEVE* and thereby walk in *Real True Faith* [full chapter in the first book]; if we learn to evaluate everything by the Word of God and The Peace that passes understanding; if we walk in proper submission to one another as coequal workers in Christ; and, if we learn how to discern and hear His Spirit versus the spirit of the antichrist,

"Beloved, do not ***believe every spirit***, but test the spirits to see whether they are from God, because ***many false prophets*** have gone out into the world. By this you know the Spirit of God: every spirit that confesses that Jesus Christ has come in the flesh is from God; and every spirit that does not confess Jesus is not from God; this is the ***spirit*** of the ***antichrist***, of which you have heard that it is coming, and now it is already in the world." (1 John 4:1-3),

then, *YES,* we can walk as our older brother Jesus did!

He showed us it was possible and how to do it. That was actually one of His purposes and goals when on earth. He meant to be our example to teach us how to walk with the Father. He said He'd send us the Helper for us to be able do the same.

"But when the Comforter (Counselor, Helper, Advocate, Intercessor, Strengthener, Standby) comes, whom I will send to you from the Father, the Spirit of Truth who comes (proceeds) from the Father, He [Himself] will testify regarding Me." (John 15:26)

So, the ***Big IF—IF*** we can mature to this point in our growth—***THEN*** we can and will learn to walk in the Spirit; individually; and then together in unison.

SOME STILL CONFUSED WILL CONTINUE TO SAY

How can we have unison if we don't have people directing the show?

If we learn how to grow into this level of maturity. To do all of these things, as mentioned, and let the Spirit of God direct the "show". Then we'll finally be able to see the whole body functioning with all the parts working together as one. Just as He intended.

As we were told in Ephesians 4, "From whom the whole body, being fitted and held together, by what ***EVERY JOINT SUPPLIES***, according to the ***PROPER WORKING*** of ***EACH INDIVIDUAL PART***." All parts functioning together.

We are called to walk together in this way—into the functioning full body, the Bride, the true Church, as ***ONE***.

I hate to be the one to tell you, but we can *NEVER* walk in unison, as the mature body of Christ, by men's authority alone—it's *ONLY* by the Spirit of God. Men's [or women's] authority has a place in the beginning—but that's not where we're to live out most of our Christian lives or end up.

CHAPTER SEVEN

WHAT HAS TAKEN GOD'S PEOPLE CAPTIVE?

EXAMPLES FROM THE REAL WORLD

MY FRIEND

I HAVE A GOOD friend, a virtuous Catholic man, who I talk with fairly regularly, but only get to see once-in-a-while since we live in different states. When visiting and talking at his home, a few months before my first book came out, discussing some subjects included in the book; he suddenly closed down. He got quite defensive, saying, "Well, I'd need to run that by the 'Deacon' first before I can discuss that."

Revealing the *Stockholm Syndrome* and a place of "safety" he could fall back on so he didn't need to confront or deal with the truths that might challenge his engrained taught *Belief Systems*. And, in actuality, was the excuse to avoid dealing with them, as I'm convinced he *NEVER* would have run them by the "Deacon" anyway.

HOW MANY OTHERS DO THE SAME?

Moving the focus of the discussion away from themselves, passing these subjects [or pretending to pass them] over to their "leaders"—so they don't need to confront their engrained *Belief Systems*.

And what happens if those leaders find out and shut it down? Never allowing those people to enter the conversation again, as with my friend along with others, we will talk about shortly.

Yes, my friend and I remain friends and can communicate on any other subject. Which we do. Just not this one. But every time after this discussion, if I ever mentioned anything related, no matter how minor, no matter how indirect about the book—*CRICKETS—GHOSTING*. Until some unknown amount of time passes. Then later we could discuss a different subject, [pretending] as if I never had mentioned the other.

DECEPTIONS HAVE TAKEN US CAPTIVE

DICK'S FAMILY REUNIONS

I talked about Dick, my spiritual father, in the first book. I was very involved and part of his family's lives for a good number of years. We didn't just go to church or home groups together, I probably lived at his house more than my own. He, his wife, Janet, and their four children, Julie, Kris, Lisa, and Richard Jr, were my adopted family.

I ate with them. Hung out with them. Spent most of my free time with them. I didn't sleep there—but I'm sure I could've of if I wanted. His children were all younger than me and were the minor siblings I never had. The three older girls were always wanting to put their makeup on me and play hairstylists with my 1970s hippy mid-back length hair.

I went on outings with them. Hand-cranked ice cream with them. Hey, I was young free labor! So it's not unusual that I went to their family reunions with them. Because I was part of the family.

About fiftyish people would gather at these reunions held somewhere in Ohio, central to Dick's brothers' families who also lived in Ohio. But the one brother from California and his family would fly in each year.

Dick's Niece

There I met many of his extended family. One of them was Dick's niece from the California bunch. I actually can't remember her name since it's been fifty-plus years ago.

One of those times, his niece asked to meet privately with my brother, Bruce, and me. Which we did. She choose an out-of-the-way location and set a time for all of us to meet. The reason: she was nineteen and pregnant—out of wedlock—and she was terrified to tell her parents; not knowing how they'd react and what they'd do.

The year was probably 1971 or 1972, and she was petrified because society categorically rejected such pregnancies then.

She asked us, no begged us, to pray that God would take away the pregnancy. We being very young in the Lord. Bruce, maybe two years old in the Lord—and me, only one-year-old in the Lord—were kind of *DUMB*. Definitely not well-experienced or well-versed yet in the scriptures in this area.

So, we prayed together with her for quite some time—maybe an hour or two—that God would "magically" somehow remove the pregnancy from inside her. It never entered my mind that this would end a life. We didn't think of it as an abortion. As I said, we were oblivious and just *DUMB*. We just felt the pain of our sister (in the Lord) so we prayed just as she wanted.

The next day, she contacted us before heading back to California with her family and told us she had a miscarriage overnight. She thanked us so, so much—*now her secret was safe;* she'd never have to tell her parents; she'd never have to tell anyone.

In that moment, it finally dawned on me that our prayers had caused the miscarriage and taken a precious life. *I FELT AWFUL.* That's not what I meant. But I'm just not sure what else was supposed to happen. Just *oblivious* and *DUMB*.

Now as I look back on it, I'm sure that God did *NOT* answer those prayers—but the *god* of this world, he with the little "g" was glad to do it. You can read all about why and how we as "good Christians" can be a vessel for evil when we don't know how to pray correctly—as told in the first book.

What's even more tragic was on the exact day one year later she committed suicide—because of aborting her child. As many women have done on the anniversary of their abortions.

I don't know what anyone really knew. I don't know if she'd told her parents before then or if she left a note. But since Dick knew I'd known her from the reunions, he told me she'd committed suicide. Now I felt much, much worse. I never told Dick or anyone else about all of this—*EVER*—until you're reading about it now.

I lived with tremendous guilt over this for many years—always haunting me from the deep recesses of my mind; but never allowing it to be brought forward. Unfortunately, unknowingly, I allowed this shameful incident to take ownership of a piece of my mind and hold me captive for all those years.

Twelve-year-old Cousin

Shortly after her death—I can't remember if it was some months or a year later—one of the young cousins, a boy, maybe twelve years old, died. I can't remember what he died from. He was the son of one of Dick's other brothers that lived in Ohio.

As an "adopted" honorary member of the family reunions, Dick invited me [wanted me] to come to the funeral—he instructed me to come to his house and then ride there with his [my "adopted"] family. He strongly insisted.

For two or more solid days before the funeral, I was under *TERRIBLE* guilt, shame, and fear. Was I still being haunted from the recesses of my mind about Dick's niece? At that point in time, I wasn't sure—but that could've been a big part of it. Nevertheless, this time I believed the Lord was telling me to go to the funeral home and, during the viewing, pray over the boy in his casket to raise him from the dead.

We know Jesus raised Lazarus from the dead. We know the disciples prayed over Paul and he came back to life after being stoned to death. In the same way, back in those Charismatic days, we were also hearing of the dead coming back to life as Christians prayed. So, the request did not seem unbelievable.

I didn't sleep at all during those two or three days. I lived under an overwhelming pressure I couldn't handle as a two-year-old Christian. I prayed constantly to find out if I was really supposed to go. I thought I was hearing I should do this thing. But I couldn't do it. The pressure was too great. What if I prayed and nothing happened? How foolish would I look in front of Dick and all of his family?

But what if I did, and the boy was raised from the dead [after being embalmed]? Oh, how amazing!

[Pretending I'd have no pride afterwards] "Oh how wonderful everyone would think of me", and, "Duh, of course, only as a servant of God". How *DUMB* we act and fool ourselves.

That day, I didn't go to Dick's house. I never attempted to go. I likely fabricated an excuse about being sick. The days of sleep deprivation and fear probably resulted in sickness and exhaustion for me.

While I knew God could use Dick or any other Christian there to raise him

SET THE CAPTIVES FREE

from the dead, I wrestled with the voice and its instructions for all of those days. I heard that "God" *ONLY* wanted me to do it and if I didn't obey Him, that the boy wouldn't be raised. This made the pressure even worse.

It ALL depended on me.

I didn't go, and no one raised the boy from the dead. Oh, how that multiplied my guilt that would haunt me and hold me captive for many years.

What I learned many years later when praying and the Lord brought up these events to me for my internal healing: First, I was being "played" [deceived] by the wrong spirits on all sides. Ambassadors [fallen spirits] from *god*, he with the little "g". Second, I was under such guilt about Dick's niece I *NEVER* could have heard correctly about the funeral incident. Third, if God really wanted to raise this twelve-year-old boy from the dead—He would've done it. He did *NOT* need me. It *NEVER* depended on me. As said, He could've just as easily used Dick or many other believers there that day. So I was inconsequential to His plan—even if that had been His will.

Listen closely.

When you hear you're the *ONLY* one who can do this—because God *ONLY* ordained you for this moment—***IT'S PURE BS***. It's a lie straight from the pit of hell. Sorry, you or I are just not that important. Just another deception played out on our egos.

Again, unfortunately, I allowed this sad incident to take ownership of a piece of my mind and hold me captive for many years.

FALSE CHRISTS, FALSE ANOINTINGS, FALSE PROPHETS, FALSE

APOSTLES, FALSE LEADERS

Do you remember the extensive discussion on false Christs, false anointings, false prophets, false apostles, and false leaders from the first book?

Let's Review False Christs and False Anointings

"For false Christs [messiahs] and false prophets will appear and show [perform] great signs and wonders to lead astray [deceive], if possible, even the elect." (Matthew 24:24; Mark 13:22)

What is a false Christ? Is it someone who goes around and says, "I'm Jesus Christ"? How many people, especially Believers, would be led astray or deceived by that? Not many, I hope, especially the elect (yielded Believers).

Oh, but you say he or she is performing signs and wonders. Okay, that might deceive a few more, but don't magicians do the same? Who knows, maybe he or she could influence some more—but probably still few in total.

What would deceive the many?

Do you remember the Greek definition for Christ is "the Anointing?"

So a *false Christ* is a *false anointing.*

NOW THAT'S A DIFFERENT STORY!

That's a RECIPE for disaster.

False anointings could deceive Believers and, possibly, even the elect.

How is a false anointing created in or around a person? Who would empower such an anointing?

The *god* of this world, the deceiver, the one who loves to lie, manipulate, and lead astray the people of this world. Don't you understand by now, as the most powerful being God ever created, he can manipulate a hell of a lot? And what he cannot manipulate directly, he can direct his minions to do for him, including performing signs and wonders.

Do you remember when the Pharisees accused Jesus of being Beelzebub (one of the many names of the devil)? "The Pharisees said, 'It's by Beelzebub, the prince of demons, that he drives out demons.'" (Matthew 9:34) Yet, we know that Jesus really cast out demons.

So why would they say that?

Because they understood the devil can simply command his demon underlings to come out of someone anytime, he wants—immediately—all for "show and tell"; performing fake exorcisms and fake healings.

Now those are signs and wonders that might even deceive the elect.

How do we test for false anointings versus the real?

Once again, *ONLY* by *THE PEACE* of God that passes understanding (Philippians 4:7). Satan can fake a lot, but he cannot fake *"THE PEACE."*

As we already saw in First John 4:1,

"Beloved, *DO NOT BELIEVE EVERY SPIRIT*, but *TEST* [analyze, examine] the *SPIRITS* to see whether they are from God..."

We are to evaluate everything *by THE WORD* of God and *HIS PEACE* together—not just the Word by itself—that's not enough; remember the enemy knows the Word of God better than us.

Remember the "OFF" feelings and "CHECK in the spirit" we discussed earlier?

That's the polar opposite of *HIS PEACE that passes understanding*.

These are the warnings from the Holy Spirit inside (ALL of) us, as Believers, trying to keep us from falling for the *false Christs* and *false anointings* that come from the "Priests of God" and their [*Stockholm Syndrome*] converts in the demons-in-nations' *false Belief Systems*.

Let's Review False Prophets

Again, from the first book:

What's a prophet?

The word *prophet* [in Latin] breaks down into two parts—"pro" which means "forth" and "phet" which means to "speak"—therefore, the word *prophet* means to "speak forth."

The part of First John 4:1 I left out from above, was *"BECAUSE MANY FALSE PROPHETS* have gone out into the world." In whole, it says, "Beloved, *DO NOT BELIEVE EVERY SPIRIT,* but *TEST* [analyze, examine] the *SPIRITS* to see whether they are from God, *BECAUSE MANY FALSE PROPHETS* have gone out into the world."

Ezekiel 13:3–6 says,

"This is what the Sovereign Lord says: woe to the *FOOLISH PROPHETS* who follow their own spirit and *HAVE SEEN NOTHING!*

THEIR VISIONS ARE FALSE and *THEIR DIVINATIONS A LIE.*

Even though the *LORD HAS NOT SENT THEM,* they say, *'THE LORD DECLARES,'* and expect Him to fulfill their words."

So, let's discuss what is a false prophet. He or she is someone under the influence of a *false Christ* (a *false anointing*). Make sense?

False Anointings Create False Prophets

A prophet of God, under God's Anointing, speaks forth the *CURRENT*

WORD of the Living God.

Conversely, a false prophet speaks forth the deceptions of *false Christs* and *false anointings.*

"YOU WILL KNOW THEM BY THEIR FRUITS. Every good tree bears good fruit, but the bad tree bears bad fruit ... thus, by *THEIR FRUIT, YOU WILL RECOGNIZE THEM."* (Matthew 7:16–20)

So be warned: Don't let yourself be deceived by everything you hear. Once again, test it by *THE WORD* of God and *HIS PEACE* that passes understanding together.

Note: Wolves in Sheep's Clothing and Charlatans are the same as false prophets—just hiding under different pretexts—typically operating differently than a "prophet." Therefore, they can be more deceptive and convincing to the masses simply by not declaring that they are "prophets."

Colossians 2:8 says,

"See to it that no one takes you **CAPTIVE** through **HOLLOW** and **DECEPTIVE PHILOSOPHY,** which **DEPENDS** on **HUMAN TRADITION** and the **ELEMENTAL SPIRITUAL FORCES** of this **WORLD,** rather than on **CHRIST** [on *the **Anointing**]."*

Someone declaring themselves to be a "prophet" would and should receive more scrutiny. Instead, these folks might portray themselves as "do-gooders," tugging at your heartstrings, maybe wanting, begging for donations for some "worthy cause" that actually just lines their pockets. Maybe a purveyor of missions—pushing some "spiritual-sounding" agenda.

Maybe a pastor, a teacher, a minister, or someone doing some "ministry from or for God." While sounding good on the surface, it's built to lead you down the wrong path for many reasons. Don't get me wrong, there are some good people doing some good things, but there are evil-backed ones doing others.

Remember Ephesians 4:14 tells us,

"We are *NO LONGER TO BE CHILDREN*, tossed here and there by waves, and *CARRIED ABOUT* by every *WIND* of *DOCTRINE*, by the *TRICKERY* of *MEN*, by *CRAFTINESS* in *DECEITFUL SCHEMING.*"

And in Matthew 7:15, we're told,

"*BEWARE* of the *FALSE PROPHETS*, who come to you in *SHEEP'S CLOTHING*, but inwardly, are *RAVENOUS WOLVES.*"

False Anointings Create False Apostles and False Leaders

Paul instructs us about such in Second Corinthians 11:13-15:

"For such men are **false apostles** [spurious, counterfeits], **deceitful workmen**, masquerading [disguising themselves] as **apostles** (special messengers) of Christ (the Messiah).

And it is no wonder, for Satan himself [**disguises**] **masquerades** as an angel of light;

So, it is **not surprising** if **his servants** also **masquerade** as **ministers** of **righteousness.**"

And again, let's review false apostles and false leaders (in conjunction with false prophets), from the first book.

Remember, "*UNTIL*, and *ONLY*, *UNTIL*" we just talked about?

Where apostles, prophets, evangelists, pastors, and teachers are typically referred to as the fivefold ministries and the fivefold's job is an "*UNTIL ministry.*" But as mentioned, some still wanting to retain power will argue that "attaining to the unity of the faith" is a lifetime process. Therefore, their job (and power and control) will *NEVER* be done.

Which is flat out FALSE.

It's a false statement wanting Believers to remain under their power and control.

As stated in the first book, the fivefold must position themselves at the bottom of the bottom, to support the Saints, to lift (build) them up, and do *EVERYTHING* possible to *WORK THEMSELVES OUT OF A JOB.* Then they are functioning *IN CHRIST* (in *the Anointing*).

If not, then they're operating under *false Christs* and *false anointings* making them *false apostles, false prophets, false evangelists, false pastors, false teachers,* and *false leaders.*

Not Everyone Who Says to Me 'Lord, Lord'

"Not everyone who **says** to Me, *'Lord, Lord,'* will enter the Kingdom of Heaven, but he who **does** the **will** of My Father who is in Heaven will enter.

Many will **say** to Me on that day, *'Lord, Lord,* did we not PROPHESY, in YOUR NAME, and, in YOUR NAME, CAST OUT DEMONS, and, in YOUR NAME, PERFORM MANY MIRACLES?'

And then, I will declare to them, 'I never **KNEW** you; depart from Me, you who practice lawlessness.'" (Matthew 7:21–23)

Don't mistake my concerns here. There certainly are good people doing some of these functions or ministries for good, but here, we're differentiating the bad from the good in order to keep true Believers from being deceived.

So REJECT...

Again, from the first book.

REJECT false Christs:

Replacing the word *Christ* with *anointing*, it becomes much easier to understand. Therefore, *REJECT false anointings.*

REJECT false apostles and false prophets:

False apostles and *false prophets* are based upon and promoted by *false anointings*. Therefore, *REJECT* them. Also, reject wolves in sheep's clothing and charlatans as *false prophets* in disguise.

REJECT men or women who want power and control:

People who think they are, or others exclaim as, "God's gift."

They're NOT.

That's just a bunch of BS.

Just because God gives gifts to men and women doesn't mean they're something special or deserve it. On one hand, God gives gifts to ALL His people. First Corinthians 12:4–11 says,

"Now there are varieties of gifts, but the same *SPIRIT*.

And there are varieties of ministries, and the same *LORD*.

There are varieties of effects, but the same God who works *ALL* things in *ALL* persons.

But to *EACH ONE* is *GIVEN* the *MANIFESTATION* of the *SPIRIT* for the common good.

For to one, is given the word of wisdom, through the *SPIRIT,*

And to another, the word of knowledge, according to the same *SPIRIT;*

To another, faith, by the same *SPIRIT,*

And to another, gifts of healing, by the same *SPIRIT,*

And to another, the effecting of miracles,

And to another, prophecy,

And to another, the distinguishing of spirits,

To another, various kinds of tongues,

And to another, the interpretation of tongues.

But one and the same *SPIRIT* works all these things,

Distributing to *EACH ONE, INDIVIDUALLY,* just as He wills."

And Romans 11:29 says,

"For *GOD'S GIFTS,* and *HIS CALL,* are *IRREVOCABLE.* He never withdraws them when once they are given, and, He does not change His mind about those to whom He gives His Grace, or to whom He sends His call."

What Does it Mean that God's Gifts are Irrevocable?

It means they're binding.

Irreversible.

Final.

Unalterable.

Unchangeable.

"He never withdraws them when once they are given."

But, isn't this just another one of God's *NEGATIVE* statements? Why would someone say they're "irrevocable?" Does that suggest that revocation might be appropriate in some or many instances?

YES.

If it depended upon us and our "good works," they should. Knowing this, never magnify people or gifts. People don't have the gifts because they're "special." They have them because God gave them, and He never took them away no matter what, even if they *listened*, *followed*, and *functioned* out of the *wrong* (false) *anointings*. Therefore, never think too highly of people or their gifts.

Therefore, Be Wary

Be wary that no matter how "good" or "spiritual" or "righteous sounding" any of these things may seem—the *god* of this world will use *ALL* of these avenues of *deception* to *take* and *keep* God's children *Captive*—to cause them to miss out from God's intended intimate relationship with Him.

SOME OF THE GREATEST DECEPTIONS ARE WITH SPIRIT-FILLED BELIEVERS

Sometimes, the worst deceptions afflict Baptized in the Spirit, Spirit-filled Christians.

Why?

Because now they've tasted some amazing things in the spiritual realm that they *NEVER* knew existed before. Which not only opened them to hear from the Holy Spirit, but now also the wrong spirits, as we saw and discussed previously from First John 4.

Now they know they can experience the spiritual realm in a *NEW DYNAMIC WAY* of living.

However, untrained individuals, ignoring God's explicit instructions in His Word and pursuing spiritual experiences improperly, leaves them vulnerable and can easily fall prey to deception—and the deceiver eagerly awaits such opportunities.

We see in Ecclesiastes 4:3,

"But better than them both [I thought] is he who has not yet been born, who has not seen the evil deeds that are done under the sun."

Could that also translate to being born [filled] by the Spirit?

I'd infer that for today, considering this subject, it would be better to have **NEVER** tasted the things of the *spiritual realm* than fall under the **DECEPTION** of evil.

This is where even dedicated Believers, if untrained, thinking they are hearing from God, can create some of the **Greatest Deceptions** in the Church.

Let's be clear, some do hear from Him.

But, some don't.

Even worse, are the ones hearing some *"strange (unholy) mixture (or fire)"*. Unfortunately, many are hearing from the *god* with the little "g" who is just waiting for his chance to throw Believers off God's intended path in order to take them down.

This is a place where *INSANITY* can happen—people hearing voices. If left untrained, partially trained, or biased trained [by *false Belief Systems*]; if not rightfully trained by The Spirit of God through a deep, balanced study of God's Word; then we will see once again,

"Beloved, **DO NOT BELIEVE EVERY SPIRIT**, but **TEST** [analyze, examine] the **SPIRITS** to see whether they are from God, **BECAUSE MANY FALSE PROPHETS** have gone out into the world."

You need to understand something here. We were *ALWAYS* hearing voices (previously)—actually it's been true for all our lives—we just didn't know it. Yes, we were continually hearing from demons ["the devil on one shoulder"] or from the Spirit of God ["angels on the other shoulder"]—but we just assumed those were our own thoughts. Now that your eyes are being opened to the truth, here and from the first book, you need to deal with these truths—and, unfortunately, "you can't unring the bell" on this one.

Therefore, commit yourself to God to be trained by His Spirit.

A SAD EXAMPLE: THE IMPETUS TO WRITE THIS BOOK

The motivation (I believe came from the Lord) to write this book has to do with two great Christian sisters. I had started writing my next intended book, ***BREAKING THE CURSE OF THE GENERATIONS***, but the Lord stopped me after the following incident and redirected me to write this book first.

Some months ago, on a Tuesday, I did a Zoom podcast pre-interview meeting with two wonderful Christian ladies. The main podcaster who's been a Christian for over thirty years, being the co-pastor of her church (with her husband), and her assistant. In the Zoom were eight other Christians, besides myself, interviewing to see if we would be a fit for their Christian podcast.

All went very well. We all had some time, maybe five to ten minutes each, to share a bit about who we were and what God had put on our hearts to talk about, if selected for their podcast.

I shared a bit from the first two chapters of my first book on my cancer, how I got it, what I went through, and how the Lord healed me. Then, also, about how the Lord "graciously" brought me to an end of myself and broke me of all my religiosity and fake spirituality. All seemed touched and moved in the Spirit. The main podcaster said very positive things. She invited all of us to come do one of their weekly podcasts with her over the next couple of months.

The next day [on a Wednesday], I received the email to sign up on their calendar, but to complete it, I needed to fill out their online form. I tried to sign up for a time a few weeks later, but by the time I'd filled it out and submitted the form, those time slots were gone. So, it was either do it that night or wait a few months.

Even though I really didn't have any time to prepare, I signed up to do it that night—because the launch of my first book was already scheduled before their next time slots down the road. In the online form, I gave them several topics and quotes from the book for them to use as "starters."

The Zoom podcast interview went extremely well. We recorded for nearly an hour and a half, and their elation was evident. So much so, they said they wanted me to come back each quarter (with no end in sight) to talk about the many, many things the Lord has done and will do, all included in my book.

The following day, her assistant sent me an email with the link for the next quarter. I immediately signed up online and she and the main podcaster both replied in excitement, confirming the date. The ladies and I quickly exchanged many emails. They both exclaimed how excited they were about the first interview and *ALL* to come every quarter down the road. They couldn't wait!

In the first interview, we covered many wonderful things about walking with the Father as being the *MOST IMPORTANT* thing we can do before ever worrying about anything else, including standing in God's Authority (which is also important). We also discussed forgiveness [from the book] and how important that subject is for all of us.

The podcast was supposed to be aired four days later on the following Sunday morning.

But it wasn't.

I checked on all the podcast channels they'd originally given and their Facebook page that showed all podcasts from each Sunday.

Nothing there.

On the next day [Monday] I checked everywhere, again, in case I'd missed it. When I couldn't find anything, I emailed both asking them when I could find it on the two largest podcast channels they used, Amazon Music and Spotify, as well as others. Asking why it wasn't up on any of the many formats they said it would be.

But this time there was *NO* response—*which was strange.*

Remember, just the week previous, building up to and through the interview, I had daily, maybe multiple times a day, extremely quick responses, full of excitement.

This time, "CRICKETS."

Out of concern, I prayed for them, for their safety; standing for whatever was going on. I continued to do so daily for the next week. During which I emailed both several times with *"CRICKETS"* in return.

Was I being "GHOSTED?"

But, Why?

As I continued to pray for them, I believe the Lord showed me they had fallen under the "spell" warned about in First John 4:1, "listening to and believing the wrong spirits."

YES, this can happen to good Christians.

And, unfortunately, it happens far too much.

Shouldn't Christians know better?

YES.

Shouldn't Christians be protected from such?

Unfortunately, not.

We Only See in Part and Know in Part

Let's revisit First Corinthians 13:12 from earlier, where we read in the AMP:

"For *NOW* we are *looking* in a *mirror* that gives only a *dim (blurred) reflection* [of *reality* as in a *riddle* or *enigma*], but then [when perfection comes] we shall *see* in *reality* and face to face! *NOW* I *know* in *part (imperfectly),* but then I shall know and understand fully and clearly, even in the same manner as I have been fully and clearly known and understood [by God]."

This verse is far too important to gloss over. Many want to think and say that they "hear from God", as if they have the direct line to Him, and can hear, see, and know *SO MUCH MORE, SO MUCH BETTER, SO MUCH CLEARER* than the rest of all us "common folks."

Yet, can't we ALL can hear from God?

YES.

You can study this in greater detail in the first book. But how well can *ANYONE* see, hear, and know Him?

All of Us Are Limited, by Design

So, to the many who say that they "hear from God", have a direct line to Him, and can hear, see, and know *SO MUCH MORE, SO MUCH BETTER*, and *SO MUCH CLEARER* than the rest of us, or even allude to such are *"HIGH"* or *"DRUNK",* sucking on their own *"EGO JUICE"*—poured out by the *god* of this world.

This is the time to understand that we must *ABIDE* in genuine humility before God (again covered in the first book in great detail). Unless you humble yourself before God, recognize you are weak, without power in yourself, *ONLY* able to *HEAR, SEE,* and *KNOW IN PART* [AT

117

BEST—EVEN ON OUR VERY BEST DAYS], as just described, then you will fall and you will fail.

Back to the Two Sisters

This is *the part I sensed;* I believe the Lord showed me (in part, since we *NEVER* know it all—as we just learned) that they had been listening to two different sources who were speaking into and swaying their minds.

The First Source

The first was another interviewee that had been on the eleven-person Zoom call the Tuesday night before the podcast recording. I had been in contact with him and his producer several weeks previously via another Zoom call and continued communicating via email to prepare for their podcast.

Originally, they had been extremely excited [like the two sisters], during their Zoom interview discussing some of the same things and unequivocally wanted me to do an upcoming podcast with them. Actually, I was already scheduled for that podcast for the week following the Zoom with two sisters.

I found them a bit "odd" and was concerned over some of their posturing, like saying they thought the Lord wanted them to change their names. That hit me as "very strange" at the minimum. And the names they told me were actually even much stranger.

It wasn't like they wanted to change their name from Jacob to Israel [meaning "wrestled with God"], as God did after Jacob wrestled with an angel all night, nor as Saul changed his name to Paul [meaning "little"—like God was humbling Saul for the proud Pharisee he'd been]. And, to the contrary, Paul was actually already his Roman name (being a Roman citizen), as well as him having the Hebrew name, Saul. Those being the only two times I can remember name changes in the Bible.

Actually, it reminded me of my old "spiritual weirdo" days and early stages in growth—but even in my worst "spiritual weirdo" days [as told in the first book] I didn't act that crazy.

I gave them my book in both electronic and audio forms so they could better understand my experiences and scriptural background to curate questions for their upcoming interview with me. All was going great with them—having good and continuous communications.

Then three days after the eleven-person interview and two days after the podcast with the two sisters, they contacted me to say "They didn't think we were a good fit.", and that in reading my book, "What I had was too mature for their audience of younger believers.", and "After further review of your book, we have determined that it is more suited for a mature Christian audience. Given that our audience comprises individuals from various faith backgrounds and many new Christians, we believe it would not be a suitable fit.", and "Therefore, we have decided not to proceed with the recording. We pray you understand our decision, and we also pray for your continued success."

Sounded like pure BS.

Since all had been going so well for several weeks with them. Instead, it sounded like the interviewee [podcaster] didn't like what I said to the ladies, or something else was definitely going on. Following the name change comments and then expressing fear that I would speak to their "younger audiences", I can only speculate as to the reasons for this fear—as my mind considers the worst.

I graciously accepted their rejection and sent them an email blessing them, stating (and sincerely meaning), "Not a problem. Hope all is well and goes well for you both."

I sensed that he had reached out to the ladies, filled them with his bias against me from something they'd read in the book, and then spoke ill of me into their ears. What, I don't know, nor do I care to know.

I also remember him talking a lot about a particular sin area that he'd just overcome after thirty years. I felt like it might still be an area he still struggles with, as we all do, in some area or another. So, no condemnation or judgement at all. His continued overemphasis of it reminded me of national-level well-known preachers who continuously used to preach hard against adultery, fornication, pornography, or other sins to only find out later that they were doing those same things—being held captive under those sins.

As we've already discussed, it's not about the sins. It's about if we're yielding ourselves to the only one who can help us walk through and beyond those sins. Then not allowing *SIN* to take ownership of a piece of our minds, hold us captive for many years, and make us miss out on the intimate fellowship we could've had with the Lord during all that time.

We would *ALL* do well to remember when, "The teachers of the law and the Pharisees brought in a woman caught in adultery. [They were trying to trick Jesus] But Jesus said to them, 'Let any one of you who is without sin be the first to throw a stone at her.'" (John 8:3,7)

The Second Source

The second part I sensed that (again) I believe the Lord showed me was about "their Bishop."

As I mentioned, the main podcaster has been a Christian for over thirty years and is the co-pastor of her church. Before we started the interview that Wednesday night, she told me many things about her struggles in her thirty-year walk and how she and her husband had come through all of it and were now co-pastoring a church in a small town in Ohio. She mentioned they were under a "structure of leadership" from Columbus and directly under "the Bishop."

When she said it, it felt very *"OFF"*—I had a *"CHECK in the spirit"*—but I let it slide as the two of them seemed like wonderful sisters and we were about to start the interview.

What I sensed was that they took the (tainted) information from the interviewee, above, along with reading excerpts from my book—most likely some of the controversial portions that challenge LEADERS and church religiosities and then talked to "the Bishop." I sense he gave a very negative reaction, maybe decried "heresy" and "heretic". Then he strongly said, "NO.", "Have nothing to do with him.", and "They should drop me." So they did. Never to hear from them again.

As I prayed for them daily, my last email to them, sent a couple of weeks later, is shown here exactly as it was originally sent, except I have asterisked their names to avoid embarrassing them publicly.

P***** and D*******,

So, it's been 2 weeks since we had the Zoom podcast interview together. I thought we all had a great time together that night. And I felt that seemed true for all 3 of us. So much so, that the next day you had me sign up for the discussed/planned quarterly podcasts.

Yet, for some reason you did not put up my podcast interview anywhere even though your FB page said it would happen (that you should take down if you changed your minds). And unfortunately, when I emailed you both the 2 times previous last week, I got "crickets".

I'd love for you to be honest & tell me if I said and/or did anything wrong in that interview that night. Or for what horrible reason you have ghosted me? If I did anything wrong, I sincerely apologize to you both & I welcome corrections so I don't ever make the same mistakes in the future.

I think you both are wonderful Christian sisters & am actually concerned for you (that we can discuss further if you desire at some other time). But you do need to know that it is not only unprofessional in any type of business world (Christian or secular) to ghost someone, but also, it's certainly not Christ-like which is a higher standard we are held to by the Lord. Therefore, I would highly recommend that you not only correct this situation, but never do that again to anyone else in the future.

As I said please be so kind to get back w/me & give me an honest full review especially if I did or said something so wrong it resulted in your choice to ghost me.

And until I hear otherwise, unfortunately, I'm assuming that you're backing out of doing the discussed/planned quarterly podcasts. Just so you understand, neither the recorded podcast or the future ones are what's the most important issue here.

With all respect & hoping you will do the right thing in spite of how difficult it might be,

Tom

Even after that—CRICKETS.

As I continued to pray, I believe the Lord showed me because He loves them so much that they will need to go into the wilderness (for however long it takes for them) to break free from the Bishop and their *false Belief Systems.* I really hope to hear a wonderful report from them one day about how God brought them through.

By the way, I don't blame them at all. They were simply *Stockholm devotees* following their training.

FINAL THOUGHTS

Immediately after the great podcast recording we did on that Wednesday,

I gave them a pre-release copy of my book to read and the audio version to listen for the upcoming quarterly interviews. I also gave them a warning that there might be some "difficult things" for them to hear—and if they found that to be true, I said just "eat the meat and throw out the bones." I gave them that caution because I know my book *STRONGLY* challenges the status quo and many leaders in the churches, no matter how *SPIRITUAL* they think they are with God.

I sense they got (stuck) no further than chapter two, which is just the beginning of such challenges in the book—and they couldn't handle them because of their full-time residence in their *false Belief System.*

Do you remember in the chapter on "AREAS OF CAPTIVITY", when we discussed being held captive by a religious spirit? I believe this is another example where the two wonderful Christian sisters fell captive again—most likely brought into their lives, by osmosis, as acceptable behavior from "their Bishop" and *Belief System.*

So, when you put all of these things together, it became the "perfect storm" for the ruler of this world to use First John 4:1.

After praying for many days on this and for their wellbeing—wanting the best for them to get past this—and not fall into the enemy's trap since they are wonderful sisters; I sent the last email, above. They are such fine sisters; I didn't want to see them have to go waste (a lot of) time in the wilderness before they can eventually find their way back. But sometimes we must accept that we cannot rescue good people from needing to go through the wilderness. Which I have full confidence in the Lord that they will come through on the other side and much better for the experience—hopefully free from *Captivity.*

It's just a shame they [or us or anyone] must waste so much time and go down that path. But it's not my job, nor anyone else's, to "save" or rescue them from it. We can only throw out the lifeline. Others must choose to grab on or not. Yet, it's God's faithfulness to take us through such so we can *LEARN* not to give in and repeat the same mistakes, again, the next time. Sometimes it takes going to hell and back.

As Deuteronomy 29:29 says,

"The *SECRET THINGS* belong to the LORD our God,

But the things *REVEALED* to us, belong to us, and our children, forever

So that we may *FOLLOW* [observe] *ALL* the words of His [law] directions, instructions, teachings, and rulings."

Until they go through it, and get God's *REVELATION* about these matters, they *MUST* live in the wilderness until able to *FOLLOW* [observe] *ALL* the words of His directions, instructions, teachings, and rulings.

I was hoping upon hope that they would've at least responded with a "dear John" type letter I could've gently challenged—so they wouldn't need to go down that road; throwing them a lifeline with "I hear you.", "But now will you graciously and honestly tell me the complete truth of what's really going on here?" I was hoping I could get them to expand on the truth. Then I was going to say, "Yes, I saw that.", and then share First John 4:1-3 hoping to save them time in the wilderness.

As of this time, before publishing this book, that hasn't happened. Hopefully, someday.

This *EVENT* is the motivation, catalyst, and impetus (I believe from the Lord) to write this book and to move it to the front of the list of Next Books I'm doing.

Sometimes it's not the right time to say anything. But it's *ALWAYS* the right time to pray for them in the Spirit (Ephesians 6:18, Romans 8:26–27) as they go through the wilderness. Some plant, some water, some harvest. Don't worry which thing you're to do—just do as the Father, by the Spirit, tells you to do [as best you can see and hear], when He tells you. If not, just pray.

IT HAPPENED AGAIN

Shortly after this event, it happened again with another podcaster.

Right around the same time, another new podcaster from the same FB Christian Podcaster's group was very excited to interview me. I filled out her online form to do the pre-interview the next day. Both of us exchanged a lot of good info in preparation. All was "good" until one-half hour before the Zoom call—when I received a "canceled" email for the Zoom. That was strange by itself, but it included an updated time from a 90 min call to a 30 min call—that left me confused. Was it canceled or updated?

At the specified time, I got on and attempted to connect, but the Zoom ID had been "disabled." I immediately emailed her asking her to please explain what had happened and if she wanted to reschedule. Again, *"CRICKETS."*

At that point, I thought some of my challenging statements were starting to "circle around" and usurping those who are of the same *Stockholm mindsets.*

GOOD PODCASTS

Just to mention, these are the three outliers that happened in the beginning. To date, I've done many other very positive podcasts currently being published for the first book—with a good number more lining up.

OTHERS

SPIRITUAL LIFE CENTER

Somehow, I got onto someone's email list [I get on way too many, LOL] about "a spiritual life center," the next state over. The emails started off with: "Do you want to learn to hear God's voice?", "Do you want to find out how to get the Power of God in you?", "Do you want to learn how to become prophetic?" If so, come to these trainings.

BUT NONE OF THEM SEEMED "RIGHT."

THEY ALL FELT "OFF."

Then the emails moved into: "Learn from all of God's Prophets.", "Come hear from our Prophets and Apostles at our upcoming conferences and meetings.", "Come get your power.", "Come get your gifts.", "Come get power imparted into you." **NEVER** emphasizing walking with the Father, the Son, or the Holy Spirit. Just getting gifts and power from the "Spirit" and their "Prophets" and "Apostles".

From the "get go" I got a queasy feeling inside, from the Holy Spirit (and from the lack of Peace that passes understanding)—that *NONE* of this was good. I prayed for all the good, well-meaning, but easily deceived, Saints that might and would fall for such.

Never forget the influence of false spirits, false anointings, false prophets, and false apostles.

Don't get me wrong—I want the correct version of this. There are genuine prophets and apostles that are yielded to the Lord and are functioning properly, *IN Christ* [*in the Anointing*]. Refer to the differences clearly defined and explained in the first book.

Even though I'm not a prophet, I used to teach prophetic classes for many years for Believers to learn to hear from the Lord and function in and out of His Presence. You don't need to be a prophet to yield to the Holy Spirit and function in the prophetic (speaking forth His word).

One thing I've learned in fifty-plus years is that people walking in true authority from the Lord do not need to put a title in front of their name nor announce to anyone who they are to do the function that God gave them.

Did Jesus ever call himself a prophet?

An apostle?

Even a teacher?

No.

Most, if not all, people who do so are wrong.

Unfortunately, at this spiritual life center, I sense that this is, once again,

First John 4:1,3,

"Beloved, **DO NOT BELIEVE EVERY SPIRIT**, but *TEST* [analyze, examine] the *SPIRITS* to see whether they are from God, because **MANY FALSE PROPHETS** have gone out into the world... this is the **SPIRIT** of the **ANTICHRIST**, of which you have heard that it is coming, and now it is already in the world."

And Ezekiel 13:3–6,

"This is what the Sovereign Lord says: *WOE* to the *FOOLISH PROPHETS* who **FOLLOW** their own **SPIRIT** and have **SEEN NOTHING!**

THEIR VISIONS ARE FALSE and *THEIR DIVINATIONS A LIE.*

Even though the *LORD* has **NOT SENT THEM**, they say, '*THE LORD DECLARES,*' and expect Him to fulfill their words."

Regrettably, I believe these things are "at play" there—just on a very large scale. Trying to look and seem "legit"—to entice many good, well-meaning Believers who want to see the Power of God flowing through and into their lives. Don't get me wrong, I believe they are hearing and being led by the spirit. Regrettably, just he with the little *"s"*—the *spirit* of the *antichrist*. Promoting false prophets and false apostles—trying to deceive Believers, even the elect.

Unfortunately, many will be.

I pray for those Believers regularly that they sense in their heart, by the Spirit of God, the fluctuation of God's Peace that this is *NOT* correct and by the *OFF* feelings and the *CHECK* in their spirit that they must leave there—sooner than later.

I hope, pray and believe that some will.

I pray for the leaders there, also, but have less confidence believing they will give up the enticement of all the *POWER, INFLUENCE,* and *"GREAT feelings"* they get while under the deception by the ruler of this world. But God turned Saul [his Hebrew name] where he was a proud pharisee of pharisees, into Paul [his Roman name] meaning "little"; and I hope and pray for many to humble themselves to become "little" again.

Remember, people love power [as quoted earlier and from the first book]. It's a major flaw the ruler of this world knows all too well—and has used and continues to use—to seduce many to fail, even the elect, if possible.

As stated, the old saying goes, "Power corrupts, and absolute power corrupts absolutely." (Lord Acton, nineteenth-century British politician)

This is your warning: Don't get caught up in "the things of the spirit world." Get caught up in walking with the Lord.

DISTRACTIONS OF EVERY KIND

Do you remember discussing "distractions of every kind", above, with even more in the first book?

We must be on guard—at ALL times.

Watch out for the many layers and layers of gaslighting that will come at you through the power of the air—many, many, many different distractions. Distractions on every side, even valid ones—ones that will try to keep your eyes focused away from the Lord.

Remember, the enemy works with whatever works on you.

Is it fear?

Is it lust?

Is it anger, hate, wrath?

Is it temptations for money, power or control?

Is it the desire to connect with the (wrong) spirits or spiritual realm?

He knows our weaknesses, and he will use it to his advantage.

Read more on "How Does He Know What Works on You, Me, and Everyone Else?" and "What are His Goals?" from the first book.

Remember, he wants to control everyone and everything on the earth so he can take us down to hell with him and his demons on the day of judgment—which he knows is coming.

He wants to keep us from the Father.

He wants to keep us in confusion.

He wants to keep us running from one thing to the next—from one end of the spectrum to the other.

He really doesn't care what it is.

He doesn't care if its sin related.

He doesn't care if it's religion related.

He doesn't care if it's some kind of spiritual perversion.

He doesn't care how many degrees off—as long as it's anything but being 100 percent correct with the Lord.

He doesn't care if it's good, bad, or ugly.

He doesn't care if you're an upstanding citizen or the scum of the earth.

He doesn't care if you're a Christian or a non-Christian.

He doesn't care if you're a white witch or a black witch.

He doesn't care if you're into white magic or black magic of any kind.

He wants to obtain direct control by sin or by any means.

He wants to obtain direct control by getting you to yield to the wrong spiritual things—even in the churches; by adding just a little misdirection; by religion or religiosities; by "great spiritual" distractions; by denominations; by any offshoots; by any tangents, etc. No matter here, there, and everywhere.

The enemy doesn't care what we do just as long as none of us stop, repent, and ask the Lord to come into and live throughout our daily lives with Him—by His Spirit. Giving over control, yielding to Him, allowing Him to clean up our lives and get rid of the oppressing, possessing, or *false Belief Systems* that the enemy would like us to live in.

Conversely, if we learn to yield ourselves to **Christ (the Anointing)** consistently, and allow the Holy Spirit to flow through us, filling and changing these areas so that rivers of living water flow from our innermost being, he'll panic. At which point, he knows he's sunk—but rest assured, he will not quit—he will not take it lying down.

First Peter 5:8 says,

"Be alert and of sober mind. Your enemy the devil prowls around like a roaring lion looking for someone to devour."

Consequently, he will try even harder and do anything to F— us up, again.

You need to always remember what I continuously reiterated in the first book,

"We're a vessel to whomever we yield."

FALLING FOR THE THINGS THAT WILL TAKE US DOWN

If these things don't work, look for other kinds of disruptors—any kind, from any direction, at any level. Remember, he just needs to get us off by a few degrees.

What are "the things that will take us down"?

Temptation of every type of sin.

Pride.

Power.

Ego.

Control.

Lust.

(Misuse of) Sex.

(Worshipping) Money.

Anger, Hate, Wrath.

Falling for "religion" or religiosity (false religions).

Or the opposite—no religion (remembering that TRUE RELIGION is looking after orphans and widows [James 1:27]).

Falling for anything that will take our eyes off the Lord.

SO, KEEP VIGILANT

Without wisdom and understanding, you cannot be vigilant.

"Then he taught me, and he said to me, 'Take hold of MY WORDS with ALL your HEART; keep My COMMANDS, and you will live.

Get WISDOM, get UNDERSTANDING; do not forget my words or turn away from them. Do not FORSAKE WISDOM, and she will

PROTECT YOU; love her, and she will watch over you.

The beginning of wisdom is this: get WISDOM. Though it cost ALL you have, get UNDERSTANDING.'" (Proverbs 4:4–7)

With wisdom and understanding, our vigilance is to learn to avoid evil at *ALL* turns—at *ALL* costs.

Why?

Because evil *LIVES to MAKE US STUMBLE.*

"Do not set foot on the path of the wicked or walk in the way of evildoers. Avoid it, do not travel on it; turn from it and go on your way.

For they cannot *REST, UNTIL* they do *EVIL;* they are *ROBBED* of *SLEEP* till they make *SOMEONE STUMBLE.*

They eat the bread of wickedness and drink the wine of violence. The way of the wicked is like deep darkness;

[Even] they do not know what makes them stumble." (Proverbs 4:14–17, 19)

Therefore,

"Above all else, *GUARD* your *HEART,* for *EVERYTHING* you do *FLOWS* from it.

Keep your mouth free of perversity; keep corrupt talk far from your lips.

Let your *EYES* look *STRAIGHT AHEAD;* fix your gaze directly before you.

Give *CAREFUL THOUGHT* to the *PATHS* for your *FEET* and be steadfast in all your ways.

DO NOT TURN to the *RIGHT* or the *LEFT;* keep your foot from evil." (Proverbs 4:23-27)

And,

"Let us keep *WIDE AWAKE* [vigilant, alert, watchful, cautious, and on guard]. And, *LET* us be *SOBER* [calm, collected, and circumspect]. We *BELONG* to the *DAY;* Therefore, let us be sober, and put on the breastplate [corslet] of faith, and love, and for a helmet, the hope of salvation." (1 Thessalonians 5:6,8)

"Devote yourselves to prayer, *KEEPING VIGILANT* and *ALERT* in it with an attitude of thanksgiving; praying at the same time...so that we may speak forth the Mystery of Christ." (Colossians 4:2–3)

REMEMBER CURSE-LINKS

It's time we understood how any of the "things that will take us down", as mentioned; unholy desires and other distractions such as pride, power, the misuse of sex, falling for religion and religiosity, or falling for anything that will take our eyes off the Lord can deeply entrap us.

When we fall for any of these pitfalls, it allows a curse to attach itself to us and continuously bring evil on our lives and *keep us in captivity,* as we discussed in the first book.

REMEMBER THE POWER OF THE AIR

I already mentioned the power of the air here, previously; with much more available to be learned in the first book.

John 8:44 says,

"You belong to your father, the devil, and you want to carry out your father's desires. Not *HOLDING* to the *TRUTH,* for there is *NO TRUTH* in him. When *HE LIES, HE SPEAKS HIS NATIVE LANGUAGE,* for

HE is a *LIAR* and the *FATHER* of *LIES.*"

While the enemy loves to boom and blast his influence across all forms of communication—talk, gossip, TV, video, cable, radio, internet, etc.; he doesn't always want to make it booming or blasting.

In actuality, he advances most of his agenda by simple thoughts and quiet whispers. It's his version, or perversion, and the opposite of God's still small voice—as we've discussed voices to this point. In this way, the devil is whispering in our ears all the time, trying to lead us astray, telling half-truths—whatever it takes to get us off course.

He doesn't care how he gets us off course or how few degrees off he can get us as long as he gets us there—by hook or by crook.

Remember when the devil tempted Jesus in the wilderness after his forty-day fast in Matthew 4? The devil tried to tempt Him to fall for three lies. Jesus could tell them apart. Could we? What if we're exhausted? What if we're worn out? How about after fasting for forty days?

DIFFERENTIATING

The enemy is extremely tricky. He's the ruler of this world. He'll set up all the surrounding circumstances to prepare us for failure—then he'll deploy his "air tactics." So, how can we tell his air tactics apart from God's still small voice? Number one is by knowing God's Word—but remember, that's not enough since the devil knows it as well. And, number two, by sensing if God's Peace that passes understanding is there in our hearts, confirming it or not.

Never again ignore the *"OFF"* or *"CHECK in the spirit"* feelings you get in any situation—no matter how "spiritual" or good it's supposed to be.

Get this fixed into your mind—you or I can never beat him at his own game—*NEVER;* so learn to walk *HUMBLY* in the Spirit with the Father.

CHAPTER EIGHT

THE FALLACY OF [MEN'S] DISCIPLESHIP

TAKING ON THE FALSE BELIEF SYSTEM OF DISCIPLESHIP

THE "DISCIPLESHIP MOVEMENT" CULT

THE "DISCIPLESHIP MOVEMENT" WAS one of the two big denominations created by *MEN* [enabled by their demon rulers] in 1977 when the Charismatic movement died [see the first book]. The other movement was the "faith movement". Although both faith and discipleship possess a genuine basis in the Word, when examined according to God's definitions, these movements contain many fallacies. Ruled by MEN and their demon rulers.

We see in Mark 10:42-45,

"Calling them to Himself, Jesus said to them, 'You know that those who are recognized as **rulers** of the Gentiles **lord** it over them; and their great men **exercise authority** over them.

But it is NOT this way among you, but **whoever** wishes to become **great** among you shall be your **servant;** and whoever wishes to be first among you shall be **slave** of **all**. For even the Son of Man did not come to be served, but to serve, and to give His life a ransom for many.'"

And in Luke 22:25-26,

"He said to them, 'The **kings** of the **Gentiles lord** it over them; and those who **have authority** over them are called *"Benefactors."* But it is **not** this way with you, but the one who is the greatest among you must become like the youngest, and the **leader** like the **servant.** '"

BENEFACTORS?

REALLY?

Doesn't that sound like people captive under *Stockholm-syndrome false Belief Systems*?

Let's Discuss Authority

In Ecclesiastes 8:8-9 it says,

"No **man** has **authority** to **restrain** the **wind** with the wind, or **authority** over the day of **death;** and there is no discharge in the time of war, and evil will not deliver those who practice it.

All this I have seen and applied my mind to ***EVERY DEED*** that has been done **under** the **sun** wherein a **man** has ***EXERCISED AUTHORITY*** over another man to his ***HURT.***"

The words ***EXERCISED AUTHORITY*** in the Hebrew is 'shalat' (shah-LAHT) meaning *"to domineer," "to be master of," "gained the mastery over,"* and *"have dominion [over]."*

The word **HURT** in Hebrew is 'ra' (rah) meaning *"hurt," "distress," "misery," "injury," "calamity," "disaster," "harm," "evil," "ruin,"* and *"wickedness"* from the root word 'roa' (roh-ah) meaning *"badness," "rottenness," "[causing] sadness," "ugliness," "wickedness,"* and *"[pure] evil."*

So, when Soloman tells us that, "Wherein a man has **EXERCISED AUTHORITY** over another man to his **HURT**",

In the Hebrew he's saying when men want to **EXERCISE AUTHORITY** it means they want to **Domineer** them, to be **Master** over them, and have **Dominion** over them.

And to his **HURT,** means not only **causing them Hurt** but also causing **Distress, Misery, Injury, Calamity,** [causing] **Sadness, Ugliness,** and **Wickedness;** and **comes** from a **Place** of [pure] **Evil**.

This principle applies to **EVERY DEED** done under the sun—**INCLUDING MEN'S DISCIPLESHIP.** When men [or women] want to exert their authority over others, they're guilty of the same.

You or others might argue, "No, we've been taught [forever] that we're to be in submission to the men [or women] ruling over us in the church." and "We're supposed to be under their authority.", *"RIGHT?"*

We've been taught that it's not possible to have any authority unless you are under men's authority.

Many times, quoting Romans 13:1-3,

*"**Every person** is to be in **subjection** to the **governing authorities**. For there is **no authority except** from **God**, and those which exist are established by God.*

Therefore, whoever **resists authority** has **opposed** the **ordinance** of **God;** and they who have opposed will receive condemnation upon themselves.

For rulers are not a cause of fear for good behavior, but for evil. Do you want to have no fear of authority? Do what is good and you will have praise from the same."

Gee! Sounds like they're right and I'm wrong, eh?

Maybe, for a HOT Minute!

Let's see the context for those verses. When we continue reading Romans 13:4-7, we see,

"For it is a **minister** of **God** to you for good. But if you do what is evil, be afraid; for it does not **bear** the **sword** for nothing; for it is a minister of God, an avenger who brings wrath on the one who practices evil.

Therefore, it is necessary to be in subjection, not only because of wrath but also for conscience's sake.

For because of this, **you also pay taxes**, for rulers are servants of God, **devoting themselves** to **this very thing**.

Render to all what is due them: **tax** to **whom tax** is **due**; **custom** to whom **custom**; **fear** to whom **fear**; **honor** to whom **honor**."

OOPS!

I guess if leaders use the first three verses without the context, they could paint themselves to be the governing authorities (in the churches) from God. Unfortunately, the context clearly tells us to be subject to the governing authorities in the natural realm in the cities, states, provinces, and countries in which we reside.

So Now, Let's Find Out The Truth About Men's Authority [In The Churches]

Discipleship wants everyone to be under other men's authority—their authority. Under the guise of keeping everyone safe and accountable.

Is that the truth or BS?

As told earlier,

YES.

That would be correct in the beginning. We're to be under their authority to help protect us, shepherd us, train us, teach us, and raise us up. As long as they're operating *IN **Christ**, in the **Anointing**,* as a ***UNTIL ministry***.

Just as Paul instructed the Corinthians,

"For even if I boast somewhat further about ***our authority***, which the Lord ***gave*** for ***building you up*** and ***not*** for ***destroying you***, I will not be put to shame." (2 Corinthians 10:8)

*Otherwise, **NO**.*

Then What's Discipleship All About?

Did you know there are ***NO*** words in the Bible, in the Greek, or in the Hebrew for DISCIPLESHIP or ACCOUNTABILITY?

You say, WHAT!

I'm about to touch these leaders' *"sacred cow"* that they worship; and the *"golden calf"* that was built to tell Israel, saying, "This is your [new] God who brought you out of Egypt."

Oh, what a heretic I am now!

Jesus told us to go out and make disciples of all nations. Do you think He was indicating that He wanted us to make disciples unto ourselves? ***NO***. He was saying to go make disciples of all nations ***unto Him!***

Let's read it in Matthew 28:19-20 where Jesus said,

"***Go therefore*** and ***make disciples*** of all the nations, baptizing them in the name of the Father and the Son and the Holy Spirit, ***TEACHING*** them [being Teachers and Instructors (ONLY) to them] to **OBSERVE ALL** that I **COMMANDED** you."

The word **OBSERVE** in the Greek is 'tēreō' (tay-reh'-o) which means *"to guard," "to watch over,"* and *"to preserve."*

Jesus was instructing them [and us] to go **make disciples** of all nations for **HIMSELF (Only)** and then *(Only)* **teach** and **instruct** them to observe, to guard, to watch over, and to preserve **ALL** that He's COMMANDED us.

He did *NOT* say create disciples for men; and under their authority and power ego trips. He definitely did NOT say create a Discipleship Pyramid Scheme unto themselves. Both of those being the polar opposite of creating disciples for Jesus, *Himself (Only),* as He instructed.

Actually, when John the Baptist saw Jesus had come, he had his disciples follow Him. No man was *EVER* supposed to keep disciples to himself.

"Again the next day, John was standing with two of his disciples, and he looked at Jesus as He walked, and said, 'Behold, the Lamb of God!' The two disciples heard him speak, and they followed Jesus." (John 1:35-37)

Discipleship Pyramid Scheme

The *Discipleship Pyramid Scheme* is not the same pyramid schemes we're familiar with, where someone tries to get you to join into multi-level marketing. Instead, the *Discipleship Pyramid Scheme* is a hierarchy of authority. Back in 1977, someone or actually a small group of someone(s) made the decision that they were at the top; then decided who was at the next level below them; then who was the level below that; and the next; and so on.

This hierarchy scheme is cloaked in a *false Belief System* about authority. That no one can have authority unless you're under [their] authority—this birthed the structure.

It almost sounds reasonable on the surface.

It originated from the scriptures denoting authority, as noted above.

Do you remember in the chapter on "GOD GAVE THEM TASK MASTERS", when we talked about *Men's "Authority" Ruling in the Churches* and where we saw the *"YESs"* and the *"NOs"*? The *Discipleship Pyramid Scheme* is an extreme example of such.

Remember, the only *REAL* authority comes from God—and only when we're under His authority. It has *NOTHING* to do with men and their [very limited] authority.

What Are Real Disciples?

They are disciples of Jesus.

Luke 14:26-27 says,

"If anyone comes to Me and does not hate his [own] father and mother [in the sense of indifference to or relative disregard for them in comparison with his attitude toward God] and [likewise] his wife and children and brothers and sisters — [yes] and even his own life also — he cannot be *MY disciple*.

Whoever does not persevere and carry his own cross and come after (follow) Me cannot be *MY disciple.*"

The word *disciple* or *the disciples* in the Greek is 'mathētēs' (ma-thay-TAYS) meaning a *"disciple," "disciples," and "pupil,"* from the root words 'manthanō' (man-than'-o) and 'math' (ma-th) meaning *"to learn," "educated," "[to] find," "learned," "learning," and "[one who] receives instruction."*

In Second Timothy 2:2 we see,

"And the [instructions] which you have heard from me along with many witnesses, transmit and entrust [as a deposit] to *reliable* and *faithful men* who will be competent and qualified to teach others also."

In John 8:31,

"So Jesus said to those Jews who had believed in Him, If you ***ABIDE*** in ***MY Word*** [hold fast to My teachings and live in accordance with them], you are truly ***MY disciples.***"

In Luke 6:40,

"A ***pupil [disciple]*** is not superior to his teacher, but ***EVERYONE*** [when he is] completely trained (readjusted, restored, set to rights, and perfected) ***will be like his teacher.***"

In John 13:35,

"By this shall all [men] know that you are ***MY disciples,*** if you love one another [if you keep on showing love among yourselves]."

In Acts 11:26, we see where Paul discussed:

"And when he [Barnabas] had found him, he brought him to Antioch. And for an entire year they met with the church and taught considerable numbers; and ***the disciples*** were first called Christians in Antioch."

Again, recognizing that no one takes disciples unto themselves, we see Paul in Acts 9:25, where,

"***His disciples*** took him by night and let him down through an opening in the wall, lowering him in a large basket [for carrying provisions or grain]."

Many in the discipleship movement might like to say,

"See, Paul had his own disciples."

Therefore, it justifies our position to have our disciples, too.

GEE!

Almost sounds like they disproved my premise again, RIGHT?

Guess I must be wrong!

Nope. Actually, I'm not.

It's important to note that the Greek actually has no word for *"his"* in this verse. The Greek for *"his disciples"* actually just reads that phrase as the *singular* word, meaning *"disciples"* or *"the disciples"*, as in all the references above.

The literal Greek in Acts 9:25 actually reads,

"λαβόντες δὲ «οἱ μαθηταὶ αὐτοῦ» νυκτὸς «διὰ τοῦ τείχους καθῆκαν αὐτὸν» χαλάσαντες ἐν σπυρίδι"

Which literally translated, the text reads, "Those who received *this disciple* at night through the wall they sat down spoiled the grain."

Oops! Now that's even worse.

Now it's saying that Paul is ONLY one of the disciples—not a "benefactor"—not a "ruler" over any.

Let's hear it directly from Paul in his own words to the Corinthians:

"But I urge and entreat you, brethren, by the name of our Lord Jesus Christ, that all of you be in perfect harmony and full agreement in what you say, and that there be no dissensions or factions or divisions among you, but that you be perfectly united in your common understanding and in your opinions and judgments.

For it has been made clear to me, my brethren, by those of Chloe's household, that there are contentions and wrangling and factions among you.

What I mean is this, that each one of you [either] says, I belong to Paul, or I belong to Apollos, or I belong to Cephas (Peter), or I belong to Christ.

Is Christ divided into parts? Was Paul crucified on behalf of you? Or were you baptized into the name of Paul?" (1 Corinthians 1:10-13)

Here Paul is rebuking the Corinthians for causing dissensions, factions, and divisions among themselves, by saying they are of Paul or Apollos or Cephas; being anything except of Christ, as Jesus' disciples.

CONTINUING ON

In John 15:8,

"My Father is glorified by this, that you bear much fruit, and so prove to be *MY disciples.*"

John 15:8, in the literal Greek, reads,

"ἐν τούτῳ ἐδοξάσθη ὁ πατήρ μου ἵνα καρπὸν πολὺν φέρητε καὶ ‡γένησθε ἐμοὶ μαθηταί"

Which literally translated, the text reads, "In this, my Father is glorified, that you bear much fruit and *become MY disciples.*"

And the literal Greek for John 13:35, above, reads,

"ἐν τούτῳ γνώσονται πάντες ὅτι ἐμοὶ μαθηταί ἐστε, ἐὰν ἀγάπην ἔχητε ἐν ἀλλήλοις"

Which literally translated reads, "If all know that you are *MY disciples,* if you loved one another."

I want you to note clearly all these verses in the Greek, convey Jesus was speaking *ONLY* of making *HIS disciples* and *ONLY* to *HIM. NEVER* condoning, allowing, or suggesting that other men [and women] may create or get disciples unto themselves.

He NEVER said He wanted such.

He NEVER sanctioned such.

He NEVER supported such.

He NEVER approved of such.

He NEVER authorized such.

He NEVER permitted such.

He NEVER promoted such.

He NEVER endorsed such.

He NEVER encouraged such.

He NEVER accepted such.

He NEVER allowed such.

He NEVER commanded such.

He doesn't want any such—EVER.

So, men [and women] STOP TRYING TO DO SUCH!

GOOD LEADERS VERSUS BAD LEADERS

We just saw that the right kind of (good) leaders create disciples unto Jesus. Bad leaders create disciples for themselves.

In Acts 20:28-30 we see,

[**Good leaders**] "Take care and be on guard for yourselves and the whole flock over which the Holy Spirit has appointed you *guardians* and *overseers,* to *shepherd* (tend and feed and guide) the church of the Lord or of God which He obtained for Himself [buying it and saving it for Himself] with His own blood."

[**Bad leaders**] "I know that after my departure, *savage* and *ferocious wolves* will come [get] in among you, *not sparing* the *flock;*

Even from *among your own selves* men will arise [come to the front] who, by *speaking* [saying] *perverse* (distorted and corrupt) *things,* will endeavor to *draw away* the *disciples* after them [to their own party]."

Bad leaders, leaders of *false Belief Systems,* backed by their demon rulers, will come in to steal the flock. Saying whatever it takes to draw them away to create *disciples [Stockholm devotees]* unto their *own [selves],* their *own party [Belief Systems].*

CHAPTER NINE

THE FALLACY OF THE FAITH MOVEMENT

TAKING ON THE FALSE BELIEF SYSTEM OF THE FAITH MOVEMENT

MARK AND DIANE

I'M GOING TO TELL you a story that hurt me deeply, and still holds sadness today, for what I'm about to convey. It's about one of my best friends from many years ago, Mark.

Mark and I had been in sports together in High School, but we weren't really friends. After I met the Lord (details in the first book), another friend, Gary, introduced Mark to me as a Believer and our friendship took off in a new and exciting way. We fast became best friends.

After Mark married Diane, and I married my first wife (now my ex), we became best friends as couples. We did everything together and loved each other's company. All cherished this relationship.

Diane was a Believer, but Mark was concerned that she was only a Believer on the "surface level." He wanted more for her—a deeper, more personal relationship with the Lord—and for their marriage to be stronger together in that way.

This was in the late 1970s after the Charismatic movement broke into the two denominations, *The Discipleship Movement* and *The Faith Movement* [as already discussed]. These movements were a world apart in beliefs (*Belief Systems*). The Charismatic church we all attended had gravitated into *The Discipleship Movement,* which was sad, as the Spirit of God waned. But to be fair, the Spirit of God waned equally in *The Faith Movement,* as well.

Mark came over to our house one evening, alone. He asked for us to pray for Diane to find this deeper relationship with the Father. Mark said he'd do *WHATEVER* it took to see this wonderful life change happen for Diane. We prayed for quite some time with that very thought in mind.

Two weeks later, they rushed Mark to the hospital; he could hardly breathe or walk. Remember, this is a young man who was very strong, athletic, constantly working out, and in great shape. Doctors immediately admitted him to the ICU as his condition deteriorated rapidly. He soon became paralyzed from the neck down.

Next, because he could no longer breath sufficiently on his own, they did a tracheotomy. It took several days in this condition before the doctors could successfully diagnose his situation as legionnaires' disease. Not much information was available about legionnaires' disease, let alone a cure, as it had devastated many people back in the original 1976 outbreak.

The doctors were helpless to aid Mark. Their dim outlook was that *he'd need to just see if he could survive it*—then most likely be partially or totally paralyzed for the rest of his life. This was a second major event of a legionnaires' disease outbreak that was happening too many nationwide;

and many were not surviving it.

We were with Mark and Diane at his ICU bedside every day and night, supporting and praying for him. One evening when the girls left to get something to eat, as Mark and I were alone, he asked me why he was in this situation. "Why did God allow it?", "Why wasn't God healing him [as we were used to seeing many miracles]?"

I didn't want to say this—but I had to, "Mark, do you remember when you came over two weeks ago and asked us to pray for Diane to get a deeper relationship with the Lord?"

He replied, "Yes."

"Do you remember that you said that you'd do *WHATEVER* it took?"

"Do you see that Diane has been praying [a lot] and her relationship with the Lord is increasing?"

He howled, "BUT that better not be what's happening here. I didn't mean anything like this."

I said, "I believe it's God answering your prayers."

Now, he was angry at both God and me.

The next day, Terry and Debbie came to the ICU to see and pray for Mark. Terry and Debbie were another couple we'd all been friends with from the original church. But with the division of the two movements, Terry and Debbie had left and joined the largest *Faither Megachurch* in the Columbus area.

Terry and Debbie preached to us all the *"name it and claim it"* BS that faither's believe. They told Mark and Diane all they needed to do—was to claim Mark's healing and believe it. So, they sucked Mark and Diane into that *"fantasy Belief [System]"* and they did it—again and again and again—day after day after day.

The four scoffed at us because we refused to join their vain fantasy prayers.

Terry and Debbie left—I can't remember how many times they came back—a few, but not many, as I recollect; maybe every third day at best; *"naming it and claiming it"* each time. Yet, we stayed by Mark's ICU bedside every day—just doing regular 'ol praying, not fantasy praying, just believing the Father and asking for His will to be done—*no matter what that meant.*

About a week later, Mark began an amazing recovery, surprising the doctors. First, he started being able to move parts of his body. Soon, he could breathe on his own. Shortly after, they removed the trach. Next, he could sit up. Of course, after hearing such, Terry and Debbie came back to parade in their glory—and dance their victory dance—*"see our faith worked."*

Mark and Diane bought into all their BS.

Soon, Mark was permitted to leave the hospital. They wheeled him out in a wheelchair, as he could barely walk even with help—which I was there and gladly provided. But now the friendship was waning. There was a question if it would survive.

It took many, many months, maybe a year of rehab before Mark regained most of his abilities back. But never again to be the athlete and person of strength that he was before.

During this time, Mark and Diane left our church to go join the *Faither Megachurch* to be with Terry and Debbie. There they seemed happy—since Diane was now growing, as Mark had desperately prayed that night.

But because we wouldn't buy into the BS, nor join the Faithers, we became ostracized by them. They ghosted us before the term "ghosting" was invented. They abandoned our deep friendships as individuals, as well as couples. Eventually, they *NEVER* spoke to us again. The hurt was deeper than grieving for someone you loved who had died. Because you knew they were still alive, but wanted nothing to do with you.

VERY SAD.

THE FAITH MOVEMENT PYRAMID SCHEME

Just as in every Stockholm-syndrome *false Belief System,* the Faithers have their rules, regulations, and tyranny that they exert over their converts.

You must buy into their BS 100 percent to be accepted—not 1 percent less. But if you do, then you're heartily embraced as one of them—one of *God's ELITE.* Then, I'm sure after much training (indoctrination), you're permitted to go be an ambassador of their *Faither BS*—as Terry and Debbie did—to go make new *Stockholm-syndrome converts.*

Rinse and repeat. Rinse and repeat. Rinse and repeat.

Cheerful in chains together

Do you remember how the ruler of this earth and his rulers over nations, demons-in-nations, love to create divisions in the Church? Well, look at Terry and Debbie's influence over Mark and Diane.

Mark and Diane not only bought into their BS, but willingly became new *Stockholm-syndrome converts.* Even despite Mark's delayed healing and a year passed before he regained reasonable strength; and, to my knowledge, he never fully recovered his athletic abilities.

What was wrong?

Couldn't they just "name it and claim it" to [fully restored] health?

Maybe it wasn't all the hype they believed and claimed. Maybe this situation and partial [limited] healing was God only answering Mark's original prayer for Diane.

Eventually, after giving us a little *EXTRA* time to "come to [their version of] the light", which we would not accept as gospel, Mark and Diane ended the relationship with us. Which was most likely part of the demands put on them by Terry and Debbie, other leaders in that church, and the dictates or mandates of their newly adopted Stockholm-syndrome *false Belief System.*

CHAPTER TEN

WHY DO GOD'S PEOPLE STAY CAPTIVE?

NUMBER ONE

THE STOCKHOLM SYNDROME

W E'VE TALKED A LOT about the Stockholm syndrome up to this point.

It's the overriding force that introduces *false Belief Systems* and causes the "converted" [captured] to remain.

NUMBER TWO

FEELING "SAFE"

Of course, feeling "safe" is important to most everyone, if not all.

Again, another area we've discussed in detail to this point.

Remember the Israelites wanting to return to slavery in Egypt? Because there they felt "safe" with plenty of "meat to eat".

We all can fall for the same "safe" feelings. Whatever works on us.

NUMBER THREE

PEOPLE, THEIR INFLUENCE, POWER, AND CONTROL

While some may be more independent than others, there are people influencing most, if not all, of us at various times in our lives.

It could be parents, siblings, relatives, friends, or others. To be accepted, we succumb to their influence, power, and control. Which could be for our good, our bad, or a mixture of both.

Friends, Family, and Other Influencers

Is it your parents?

Is it your siblings?

Is it your relatives?

Is it your friends?

Is it your children?

Is it other influencers?

Can you name the ones that have influenced you for good or bad?

Are there people who "forced" their ways on you?

People love the approval, praise, and glory of men over the approval, praise, and glory of God. In John 12:42-43 it says,

"And yet [in spite of all this] many even of the leading men (the authorities and the nobles) believed and trusted in Him. But because of the Pharisees they did not confess it, for **FEAR** that [if they should acknowledge Him] they would be expelled from the synagogue;

For they **LOVED** the approval and the praise and the glory that come from men [instead of and] more than the glory that comes from God. [They valued their *credit with men* more than their credit with God.]"

NUMBER FOUR

NOT UNDERSTANDING SUBMISSION OR SUBJECTION

Understanding what submission or subjection truly means does *NOT* come naturally.

We received training, to varying degrees, from parents, foster parents, adoptive parents, or relatives as we grew up. Some, of course, had none of those, which means they may've been wards raised by the state.

In addition, many also learned it "on the streets" as they grew up, whether just playing with friends or in much more severe or dire situations.

We also learned, experienced submission or subjection growing up in schools to our teachers, at work to our bosses and, for many, to leaders in the churches.

All these experiences exerting the rule of governance. Someone was always at the top. And for most of us, we were down in the pecking order.

Therefore, it shouldn't be a surprise that most of us have tainted or screwed up views of submission or subjection.

Subjection to Leaders in The Church

In Hebrews 13:17 we're told,

*"**Obey** your **leaders** and **submit** to them, for they keep watch **over** your **souls** as those who will **give** an **account**. Let them do this with joy and not with grief, for this would be unprofitable for you."*

When we hear that quoted under *false Belief Systems,* their leaders will overemphasize *"**Obey** your **leaders** and **submit** to them, for they keep watch **over** your **souls**",* with little emphasis on the rest of the verse. They love to **quote** and **demand** that you must **obey** and **submit** to them, because, as they will say, "God clearly told you to do so here."

But let's look deeper. A LOT deeper.

Obey in the Greek is 'peithō' (pay'-tho) [used above] which means *"to persuade," "to have confidence," "listen," "obeying," "put trust [in]," and "took advice."*

Leaders in the Greek is 'hēgeomai' (hay-GEH-oh-my) which means *"to lead," "suppose," "consider," "considered," "regard," "regarded," and "thought"* from the word 'agō' (ä'-gō) which means *"to lead," "bring," "bringing," "carry," "taking," "going," and "led away."*

Submit in the Greek is 'hupeikō' (hoop-i'-ko) from the words 'hupo' (hoo-PO) [used above], which means *"by," "under," "about," "hands," "under: power"* and 'eikō' (ay-KOH), which means *"to yield," "to give way," "to submit."*

Over in the Greek is 'huper' (hoo-per') which means *"on behalf of," "for the sake of," "concerning," "more than," and "about."*

Souls in the Greek is 'psuchē' (psoo-khay') which means *"breath," "the soul," "heart," "life," "mind," and "person."*

Give in the Greek is 'apodidōmi' (ah-po-DEE-do-mee) which means *"to* *give up," "give back, "return," "[give] account," "make some return," "must pay back," "returning," and "repayment to be made."*

Account in the Greek is 'logos' (LO-gos) which means *"a word (as embodying an idea)," "a statement," "a speech," and "an account"* from the word 'legō' (leh'-go) meaning *"to say," "addressing," "asking," "claiming," "quoting," "speaking," "telling," and "thoughts."*

Expanding the Greek text of *"**Obey** your **leaders** and **submit** to them, for they keep watch **over** your **souls** as those who will **give** an **account**,"* easily yields the following interpretation.

"So, be **persuaded**, have **confidence** in, **listen** to, put your **trust** in, and **take advice**, as well as, **obey** those who've been given the *JOB* and *DUTY* to **lead**, to **suppose**, to **consider**, to **give regard**, and **given** the **thoughts** to **bring** [an account]; **submit** to them by **placing yourself** [as your hand] **inside** or **under** [the glove] as unto the **Lord**, for they keep watch **over** and on **behalf** of, for the **sake** of, **concerning**, and **about** your **souls**, your **heart**, your **life**, your **mind**, and **person**; as those who [by God's requirement on them] *MUST* **give up**, **give back**, make **some** [kind of] **return** [to God, who requires such of them], [where some kind of] **repayment** is to be made and **must** be **paid back**, [to give an] **account**; meaning they *MUST* make a **statement**, a **speech**, an **address**, [and answer all that is] **asked** [of them by God], **claiming**, **quoting**, **speaking**, and **telling all** the **thoughts** that encompass that solemn *DUTY* that was given to them."

This is not the tyrannical, unquestionable position that they'd like to promote and force you to believe.

If we're young, still in training, as disciples to Jesus, and need to be under leaders for this very purpose—not yet matured to be equal coworkers that have mutual submission to one another; then *YES,* the expanded version is how our obedience, subjection, and submission should be. Understanding that the leaders may not be tyrants, "lording it over us". They have a solemn *DUTY* before God to watch over, lead, and protect us. And God will undoubtedly hold them accountable for how they carried out that solemn duty.

God *ALWAYS* holds leaders to a higher standard—to a higher responsibility—with a higher accounting to Him.

Therefore, rest assured,

God will hold ALL leaders accountable for how they carried out those DUTIES.

Good or Bad.

Woe to those false shepherds who tyrannized His Sheep.

There will be a Day of Accounting and Reckoning.

Wives to Husbands

In the same way, "Wives, be *subject [submit]* to your own husbands, *as to the Lord*. For the husband is the *head* of the wife, as *Christ* also is the head of the Church, He Himself being the Savior of the *body*. But as the *Church* is *subject* to *Christ*, so also the *wives ought* to be to their *husbands* in *everything*." (Ephesians 5:22-24)

This word *subject or submit* in the Greek is again 'hupotassō' (hoop-ot-as'-so), and is like 'hupeikō' (hoop-i'-ko) [above], which means *"to place or rank under," "to subject," "to obey," "put in subjection," "subjected," "subjecting," "submissive," "submit."* Which is from the same prim root 'hupo' (hoo-PO), which means *"by," "under," "about," "hands," "under: power."*

Again, the simple view of submission from the Greek means "to put the hand inside or under [the glove]." Therefore, this is *HOW wives* are to be *subject* to their *husbands*, just as the *Church* is to be to *Christ*.

This is a delicate subject, especially in western-world modern-day civilizations. Where women want to be equals, or sometimes greater, to their male counterparts. This subject deserves a lot more time than I will give it here. But I will take a moment to give a clear foundation for this setting.

Some women are content to be "under" their husbands for the right reasons. Also, there are women who are happy to be "under" their husbands, but don't know why, nor can elaborate—unfortunately, they aren't in the right place with the right understanding yet.

Then there are many who are not content to be "under" their husbands for any reason. Arguing their modern-day women's lib positions of "individual freedom" from men. They aren't right either.

So, what's the right position and understanding?

Remember when we talked about, "Looking back at Authority [as taught in the first book], we determined we must put ourselves inside or under God's Authority to have Authority. From this same place under God's Authority, we can then put ourselves in subjection to one another, as *coequal* workers in *Christ.*", this is the same truth here.

Just "As the *Church* [as the body] is *subject* to *Christ* [as the head], so *also* the *wives* ought to be to their *husbands* in *everything*", this is that *coequal* place.

Yet some women will still complain that they don't want to be the "body" while the men get to be the "head". Some will say they want to be the "head"—it's just not fair.

"I thought you just said we get to be coequals."

I would say to those women, "You just don't understand how lucky you are." If you only knew better.

First, let's take a moment to realize that the *HEART* is in the body while the *MIND* is in the head. Once again, those women might decry "foul." Thinking, "See the men get to use their minds and make all the decisions."

Actually, let's stop and evaluate this further. In reality, the men should be jealous of the women.

I'd rather be the *HEART* getting to *FEEL* the *Presence* of the *Father,* then be the *HEAD* just thinking about Him. In a marriage, the women get that position, we as men, don't.

> *As a man, let me now complain and say, "That stinks!"*

As equal coworkers, I believe that men and women should operate their marriages in a fifty/fifty manner. Doing the work fifty/fifty. Making decisions fifty/fifty. But what happens when we cannot agree on something of importance that needs an immediate decision? The *HEAD* must make that final decision.

> *Oops!*

> *That sucks!*

Now the final and full responsibility falls on the men's shoulders. Sucks to be us! Because now we will bear the responsibility before God for our marriage.

Did we make the correct decisions for our families?

Remember, God *ALWAYS* holds leaders to a higher standard—to a higher responsibility—with a higher accounting to Him.

NUMBER FIVE

LEADERS

We already discussed *false leaders*, in great detail, up to this point.

False apostles.

False prophets.

False evangelists.

False pastors.

False teachers.

False elders.

False bishops.

False shepherds.

We also discussed *false anointings* and *false Christs* in great detail. We saw that *false anointings* and *false Christs* create these *false leaders*.

It's the *false anointings* and *false Christs* behind these *false leaders* empowered by their rulers, *demons-in-nations*, empowered by the *god* of this world, that keep God's people captive in their *false Belief Systems*.

The Abuse of Disciples, Saints, Believers by Their "Leaders"

This type of captivity by such leaders is *ABUSE*—many times labeled *"Church Abuse"*. The *ABUSE* by the leaders in these *false Belief Systems* is indistinguishable and no different from:

Child abuse.

Spousal abuse.

Sexual abuse.

Elder abuse.

Animal abuse.

Any and every abuse.

Same evil. Same spirits. Same yielding to the *god* of this world and his cohorts.

Unfortunately, there are untold numbers and examples of such *ABUSE* in the churches.

Do you know anyone who has been abused?

Are you one?

NUMBER SIX

PEER PRESSURE IN THE CHURCHES

Especially by *Stockholm devotees*.

These folks have become the *ambassadors* for their inductors. They've been [deeply] trained to ***enforce*** the rules, constraints, precepts, principles, and views of the *Belief Systems* that they've sworn their full allegiance to.

Devotees 'just glad to be of service to God'

It may come across as them **encouraging** you to do the right thing. But it's the peer pressure that puts you "in line" and keeps you there. All done without the leaders' direct intervention—unless needed in the end before they threaten expulsion.

Insulating the leaders from bearing the responsibility, the blame, and the need for them to do it. Therefore, it becomes a self-policed state.

After doing their job, the *devotees* will say, "They didn't need the praise of their leaders [which they loved every second when they got such].", and, "They were just glad to *'be of service to God'*".

CHAPTER ELEVEN

PROJECTING: HERESIES AND HERETICS

BREAKING THE CHAINS THAT BIND YOU

RULERS, JEWS, PRIESTS, PHARISEES, SADDUCEES, AND LEADERS

THE CHIEF PRIESTS, RULERS, Pharisees, Sadducees, and the [practicing] Jews of that time all wanted to kill Jesus—the *Real True Living embodiment* of the **Anointing [Christ]**.

In John 7:28-32,

"Then Jesus cried out in the temple, teaching and saying, 'You both know Me and know where I am from; and I have not come of Myself, but He who sent Me is true, whom you do not know. I know Him, because I am from Him, and He sent Me.'

So, they were *seeking* to *seize Him;* and no man laid his hand on Him, because His hour had not yet come.

But many of the crowd believed in Him; and they were saying, 'When the Christ comes, He will not perform more signs than those which this man has, will He?'

[*When*] the Pharisees *heard* the *crowd muttering* these things about Him, the chief priests and the Pharisees sent officers to seize Him."

In John 5:15-18, where Jesus healed the lame man by the pool at Bethesda,

"The man went away, and told the Jews that it was Jesus who had made him well.

For this *reason,* the Jews were persecuting Jesus, because He was doing these things on the Sabbath.

But He answered them, 'My Father is working until now, and I Myself am working.'

For this *reason,* therefore, the Jews *were seeking* all the more to *kill Him,* because He not only was breaking the Sabbath but also was calling God His own Father, making Himself equal with God."

In John 7:44-48,

"Some of them wanted to seize Him, but no one laid hands on Him.

The officers then came to the chief priests and Pharisees, and they said to them, 'Why did you not bring Him?' The officers answered, 'Never has a man spoken the way this man speaks.'

The Pharisees then answered them, 'You have not also been led astray, have you? No one of the rulers or Pharisees has believed in Him, has he?'"

We see in John 7:19-24, where Jesus said,

"Did not Moses give you the Law? And yet not one of you keeps the Law.

[If that is the truth] why do you seek to kill Me [for not keeping it]?

Jesus answered them, I did one work, and you all are astounded.

Now Moses established circumcision among you — though it did not originate with Moses but with the previous patriarchs — and you circumcise a person [even] on the Sabbath day.

If, to avoid breaking the Law of Moses, a person undergoes circumcision on the Sabbath day, have you any cause to be angry with (indignant with, bitter against) Me for making a man's whole body well on the Sabbath?

Be **honest** in your **judgment** and do not decide at a glance (superficially and by appearances); but **judge fairly** and **righteously**."

Note: The Chief Priests, Rulers, Pharisees, Sadducees, and the [practicing] Jews all wanted to kill Jesus because He didn't fit the constraints of their *Belief Systems*. And worse, He wanted to expose them as *false Belief Systems*.

A Prophet's Own People Reject Him

Let's look at the Samaritan woman at the well.

In John 4:39-44,

"From that city, many of the Samaritans believed in Him because of the word of the woman who testified, 'He told me all the things that I have done.'

So when the Samaritans came to Jesus, they were asking Him to stay with them; and He stayed there two days. Many more believed because of His word; and they were saying to the woman, 'It is no longer because of what you said that we believe, for we have heard for ourselves and know that this One is indeed the Savior of the world.'

After the two days He went forth from there into Galilee.

For Jesus Himself testified that a **prophet** has **no honor** in his own country."

Jesus' own people, the Jews, did not willingly accept him. The Samaritans, who did not believe they had the same rights, privileges, or heritage as the Jews, accepted Jesus more readily. Reason: The Jews' *(false) Belief Systems* constrained them.

Jesus Defines The Difference

"So Jesus said to them again, 'Truly, truly, I say to you, I am the door of the sheep.

ALL who came before Me are thieves and robbers, but the sheep did not hear them.

I am the door; if anyone enters through Me, he will be saved, and will go in and out and find pasture.

The thief comes only to steal and kill and destroy; I came that they may have life, and have it abundantly.'" (John 10:7-10)

Jesus came that we may have life and have it abundantly. But *thieves [false leaders]* only come to steal, kill, and destroy—by *false Belief Systems* rooted and ruled by their demons-in-nations.

HERETICS AND HERESIES

Let's look at some scriptures that define what are **true Heretics** and **Hersey**.

In Titus 1:10,

"For there are many rebellious men, empty talkers and deceivers, especially those of the circumcision."

Remember Paul was the first Apostle in the new Church [in Acts] that

God made as the ambassador to the Gentiles to bring them in. Paul had to stand up to the Church council and defend his position by the Old Testament. He "won" the right to say the Gentiles did NOT need to get circumcised, putting them back under the Law or worse.

Titus' concern here was that these men were pushing circumcision, under Jewish Law, and were committing **Heresy** trying to reverse what Paul had established as God's word by the Old Testament.

In Matthew 24:4-5,

"And Jesus answered and said to them, 'See to it that no one misleads you. For many will come in *MY NAME*, saying, "I am the *Christ [the Anointing]*," and will mislead many.'"

And in Matthew 24:23-24,

"Then if anyone says to you, 'Behold, here is the *Christ [the Anointing]*,' or 'There He is,' do not believe him. For *false Christs [false anointings]* and *false prophets* will arise and will show great signs and wonders, so as to mislead, if possible, even the elect."

Both verses show Jesus defining *true Heretics:* those who would come in His name and attempt to deceive many. We've discussed *false Christs* backed by the *god* of this world many times to this point.

Again from Colossians 2:8,

"See to it that no one takes you captive through **HOLLOW** and **DECEPTIVE PHILOSOPHY,** which **DEPENDS** on **HUMAN TRADITION** and the **ELEMENTAL SPIRITUAL FORCES** of this **WORLD,** rather than on **CHRIST** [on the **Anointing**]."

And remembering Ephesians 4:14,

"As a result, we are no longer to be children, tossed here and there by waves and carried about by *EVERY WIND* of *DOCTRINE,* by the *TRICKERY OF MEN,* by *CRAFTINESS* in *DECEITFUL SCHEMING.*"

And, again, from Colossians 2:20-22,

"If you have died with *Christ [the Anointing]* to the elementary principles of the world, why, as if you were living in the world, do you submit yourself to decrees, such as, "Do not handle, do not taste, do not touch!" (which all refer to things destined to perish with use)—in *ACCORDANCE* with the *COMMANDMENTS* and *TEACHINGS* of *MEN?*"

These verses give us a clear view of **true Heresies** promoted by those who preach and teach *false Belief Systems.*

In First Timothy 4:1,

"But the Spirit explicitly says that in later times some will fall away from the faith, *PAYING ATTENTION* to *DECEITFUL SPIRITS* and *DOCTRINES* of *DEMONS.*"

As we've discussed many times before, it's the demons-in-nations that rule over the churches that are the foundation for the *false leaders* who chose [on purpose or by deception] to be their mouthpieces. These *false leaders* are [prophetically] speaking forth the **Heresies** of **demons**.

Projection

The verses above help define the **true Heresies** of those who preach, teach, and promote *false Belief Systems*. The leaders who do so are the **true Heretics**, just hidden under the cloak of their self-righteous Pharisaism.

Most of the time, those who preach, teach, and decry *"Heresies"* and *"Heretics"* from the pulpit to the entire congregation and/or individually to their people are the **true offenders**. They're just **PROJECTING** their fallacies on those who challenge them and their *false Belief Systems.*

Do you remember the old saying, "When someone is pointing their finger at you, they have three fingers pointing back at themselves?"

The Pharisees considered Jesus a **Heretic**. Every time Jesus' claims or actions deviated from what the Pharisees considered being their normal, conventional, Law-based understanding, they labeled him a *Heretic*. Such as, how He delt with the woman caught in adultery, healing a man on the Sabbath, implying He was the Son of God, etc.

Some Jews considered John the Baptist a *Heretic* because he lived outside the Priests' rules and control.

Many Jews considered Paul a *Heretic* because he obeyed God and reached out to the Gentiles. This was the same hypocrisy the Jewish believers had used towards Jesus that they now were using on Paul. They didn't understand the Old Testament scriptures clearly defined God would leave the Jews behind [for a while] to reach out to the Gentiles. Paul stood before the Church council and defended his position by those same scriptures to prove he wasn't committing *Heresy*.

Nonetheless, as he informed the Corinthians, Paul and those ministering alongside him suffered even further,

"But we commend ourselves in every way as [true] servants of God: through great endurance, in tribulation and suffering, in hardships and privations, in sore straits and calamities,

In beatings, imprisonments, riots, labors, sleepless watching, hunger;

By innocence and purity, knowledge and spiritual insight, longsuffering and patience, kindness, in the Holy Spirit, in unfeigned love;

By [speaking] the word of truth, in the power of God, with the weapons of righteousness for the right hand [to attack] and for the lefthand [to defend];

Amid honor and dishonor; in defaming and evil report and in praise and good report. [We are branded] as deceivers (impostors), and [yet vindicated as] truthful and honest." (2 Corinthians 6:4-8)

They were branded *Heretics.* In dishonor. In evil reports. Branded as deceivers. Branded as impostors.

Leaders of two churches I attended declared me a *Heretic*. First by Jim, who thought himself to be an apostle. Second by Don, who probably thought he was one, too.

I had a great relationship with both men, at first, and for quite a while—years, in fact; but something changed with each. They knew exactly where I stood on every subject and why I believed such based on the scriptures. And while we may've disagreed on some things, that was totally "OK", as long as it was behind closed doors. In all those years, they *NEVER* labeled my beliefs as *Heresies*, nor did they *EVER* call me a *Heretic*.

But years later, when other members, not I, raised some of these same subjects before the entire congregation (which happened in both churches)—concerning what the leaders and I had discussed in private [with no issues]; when I stood up to side with the scriptures—I was immediately and publicly ostracized by them. In each case, shortly thereafter, each man stood up from their [bully] pulpits to declare my understanding of the scriptures as *Heresies* to protect themselves; and then called me a *Heretic* to force me to leave. Which I did.

Since: As a Believer, I refuse to stay where I'm not valued. I have *NO* hard feelings, judgements, nor unforgiveness toward them. I actually pray for blessings [*BARAK*—see the first book] upon them—and mean it. Hoping and praying that someday they will come to *KNOW* the Lord in the way we've discussed *KNOWING* [in a deep intimate way] to this point, in both books.

It's time to understand when someone or anyone challenges a "Power Structure" they will be called a *Heretic*. This is to *"PUT 'THEM'"* in *THEIR PLACE"* or *"GET RID* of *'THEM'"* or *BOTH*—to keep *"THEM"* from influencing *"THEIR"* [the "Power Structure Leader's"] flock.

Am I saying that everyone who challenges a "Power Structure" is right?

Of course not.

But should we allow everyone to challenge a "Power Structure"?

Yes!

No one is to be ostracized publicly or privately for questioning leadership—*EVER*. We must all learn to hear from the "least among us" and "from the mouth of babes". If all of us are not humble enough to learn from the least, we're being ruled by the *god* of this world. And God, He with the big "G", will humble us.

People love their "Power Structures"—especially the leaders at the "Top".

Maybe sometimes, some of these leaders are innocent—but I doubt it.

This is all part of the Rulers over kingdoms—demons over nations.

Those Who Yell The Loudest

When people call out too loudly, then most likely, they're guilty of what they're accusing others of.

Do you remember TV evangelist Jimmy Swaggart's accusations of sexual sins against everyone, only to be later found guilty of adultery himself? Do you remember the extramarital sexual and homosexual activities of TV Evangelist Jim Bakker?

These are just two examples of preachers [leaders] who used their [bully] pulpits to denounce sins but were later found to have engaged in such behavior themselves.

Remember Don, I just mentioned, above? He preached from his [bully] pulpit against lust, pornography, adultery, and other sexual sins. Of course, he made it sound "in love" to redeem God's people.

Don actually expelled his assistant pastor, a good friend of mine, because this man (I won't mention his name to ever embarrass him) had admitted to Don, behind closed doors, that he was addicted to porn. Don didn't expel him immediately—oh no. He took time to let my friend figure out how to stop. My friend would stop, and then start, and then stop, and then start again. Which is the nature of how sins work.

When Don gave him sufficient time (per Don's discretion) and my friend couldn't overcome this addiction by himself, Don called him out in front of the entire congregation and shamed him until he finally left. No, my friend didn't leave immediately, but it didn't take long.

Do you want to hear something even worse?

Some of Don's Stockholm devotees, calling themselves "prophets", pulled my friend aside and confronted him. They told him that God had told them to inform my friend he *MUST* leave the church. Yes, they heard from *god*, he with the little "g".

The sad end to this story was about another one of Don's Stockholm devotees, a woman in the church who called herself a "prophetess". She was always at Don's office "ministering to his needs". Praying over Don all the time—"because he needed so much attention" as God's chosen leader.

Later, everyone learned Don and the woman had an affair during "those office hours." Both ended up leaving viable marriages and families to marry each other. Of course, Don got kicked out of the church he'd started.

It ended with the new couple moving to another state to start—wait for it—*CHRISTIAN MARRIAGE COUNSELING.*

Can you hear the irony?

"Power Leaders" Use Fear Tactics

These leaders love to use fear tactics over their followers. The followers have witnessed them ostracizing and forcing others out they deemed *"Heretics"* or for following *"Heresies"*. These fears keep *THEIR* flocks from listening to or following others who might be there to **SET THE CAPTIVES FREE**.

The same leaders will (re)emphasize repeatedly about such *"Heretics"* and *"Heresies"* to keep the fear alive—to keep them "in line". This enables these leaders to put and keep "their disciples" under "their laws" and *false Belief Systems.*

Do you remember the two wonderful [podcast] sisters and their Bishop that I discussed earlier? They're a prime example.

Other Words

What are other words or phrases that these leaders will use to define *"Heretics"*, *"Heresies"*, and/or what they'll do to those who promote such?

Calling them Rebels.

Declaring them to be in Rebellion [which is the same as witchcraft (1 Samuel 15:23)].

Declaring them to be in Sedition.

Condemning them in front of the entire congregation.

Censuring them in front of the entire congregation.

Denouncing them in front of the entire congregation.

Banning them in front of the entire congregation and from the church.

Expelling them from the church.

Excommunicating them from the church.

Sending them to Damnation—equals cursing them.

Calling for and praying Anathemas [curses] over them.

Speaking of them or sending them into Perdition.

Therefore, if you're a *Stockholm devotee* of a *false Belief System*, wouldn't you be afraid of your leaders doing these things to you?

Most would.

Guess their plan to keep them "in line" works!

I HAVE ONE QUESTION FOR THESE FALSE LEADERS

Leaders, would you rather be called Pharisees, Sadducees, Scribes, or similar?

Jesus didn't have compliments for any.

In Matthew 23:13-33,

"But *WOE* to you, **Scribes** and **Pharisees**, **Hypocrites**, because you shut off the kingdom of Heaven from people; for you do not enter in yourselves, nor do you allow those who are entering to go in.

WOE to you, **Scribes** and **Pharisees**, **Hypocrites**, because you devour widows' houses, and for a pretense you make long prayers; therefore, you will receive greater condemnation.

WOE to you, **Scribes** and **Pharisees**, **Hypocrites**, because you travel around on sea and land to make one proselyte *[Stockholm convert]*; and when he becomes one, you make him twice as much a son of hell as yourselves.

WOE to you, ***Blind Guides,*** who say, 'Whoever swears by the temple, that is nothing; but whoever swears by the gold of the temple is obligated.'

You ***Fools*** and ***Blind Men!*** Which is more important, the gold or the temple that sanctified the gold? And, 'Whoever swears by the altar, that is nothing, but whoever swears by the offering on it, he is obligated.'

You ***Blind Men,*** which is more important, the offering, or the altar that sanctifies the offering? Therefore, whoever swears by the altar, swears both by the altar and by everything on it. And whoever swears by the temple, swears both by the temple and by Him who dwells within it. And whoever swears by Heaven, swears both by the throne of God and by Him who sits upon it.

WOE to you, **Scribes** and **Pharisees**, **Hypocrites**! For you tithe mint and dill and cummin, and have neglected the weightier provisions of the law: justice and mercy and faithfulness; but these are the things you should have done without neglecting the others.

You ***Blind Guides***, who strain out a gnat and swallow a camel!

WOE to you, **Scribes** and **Pharisees**, **Hypocrites**! For you clean the outside of the cup and of the dish, but inside they are full of robbery and self-indulgence.

You ***Blind Pharisee***, first clean the inside of the cup and of the dish, so that the outside of it may become clean also.

WOE to you, **Scribes** and **Pharisees**, **Hypocrites**! For you are like whitewashed tombs which on the outside appear beautiful, but inside they are full of dead men's bones and all uncleanness.

So you, too, outwardly appear righteous to men, but inwardly you are full of hypocrisy and lawlessness.

WOE to you, **Scribes** and **Pharisees**, **Hypocrites**! For you build the tombs of the prophets and adorn the monuments of the righteous, and say, 'If we had been living in the days of our fathers, we would not have been partners with them in shedding the blood of the prophets.'

So you ***testify against yourselves***, that you are sons of those who murdered the prophets. Fill up, then, the measure of the guilt of your fathers.

You ***Serpents***, you ***Brood*** of ***Vipers***, how will you escape the sentence of hell?"

Leaders will *NO* longer be able to hide under the *[self]* *"righteous"* cloak of being the *"most religious"* of all—the *Pharisees*. And after seeing what Jesus said about them—who would want to be?

A Word to These Leaders

If you have ears to hear and eyes to see,

REPENT.

And come back to learn, once again, how to *KNOW* *the Lord and walk intimately with Him.*

THE ACCUSER OF THE BRETHREN

In Revelation 12:7-10 we see,

"And there was war in heaven, Michael and his angels waging war with the dragon. The dragon and his angels waged war, and they were not strong enough, and there was no longer a place found for them in Heaven.

And the great dragon was thrown down, the serpent of old who is called the devil and Satan, who deceives the whole world; he was thrown down to the earth, and his angels were thrown down with him.

Then I heard a loud voice in Heaven, saying, 'Now the salvation, and the power, and the kingdom of our God and the authority of His Christ have come, for the *accuser* of *our brethren* has been *thrown down*, he who *accuses them* before our *God, day* and *night*.'"

We know the dragon, Satan, Lucifer, the devil, and his cohorts (demons) are always accusing the brethren.

So be sure that those *false leaders,* backed by their rulers, demons-in-nations, will accuse true Believers who are not giving into their lies, as well.

KILL THE MESSENGER

CHALLENGING "POWER STRUCTURES"

Those who challenge *"Power Structures"* will pay a heavy price. You must be ready and willing to be called a **Heretic** and someone speaking **Heresies**. You better be ready to be called out and ridiculed before entire congregations.

As someone who's paid that price, I'll warn you that you better have heard from the Lord—and that being He, with the Big "L"—not the *lord* of this world.

You better *NOT* be coming from a place with "an axe to grind".

You better have prayed on it many times—over and over and over again.

It's essential that you've studied the Word to be sure you're hearing correctly. You need to have a solid foundation and be ready to defend your position by the scriptures taken in context and backed by the Greek and Hebrew, if possible.

And, you better have waited until you have **The Peace** that passes understanding before you do.

But when you do, you will have Matthew 23:34-39 backing you,

"Therefore, behold, I am sending you prophets [those who **speak forth** the **living word** from the **mouth** of the **living God**] and wise men and scribes; **some** of them you **will kill** and **crucify**, and some of them you **will scourge** in your **synagogues**, and **persecute** from city to city,

So that upon you may fall the guilt of all the righteous blood shed on earth, from the blood of righteous Abel to the blood of Zechariah, the son of Berechiah, whom you murdered between the temple and the altar. Truly I say to you, all these things will come upon this generation.

Jerusalem, Jerusalem, who *kills the prophets* and stones those who are sent to her! How often I wanted to gather your children together, the way a hen gathers her chicks under her wings, and you were unwilling.

Behold, your ***house*** is being left to you ***desolate!*** For I say to you, from now on you will not ***SEE*** Me until you say, 'BLESSED IS HE WHO COMES IN THE NAME OF THE LORD!'"

OFFERING SERVICE TO GOD

"They will put you out of (***expel*** you from) [make you ***outcasts*** from] the synagogues;

but an hour is coming when ***whoever kills*** you will ***think*** and ***claim*** that he has ***offered service*** to ***God***.

And they will do this because they have not ***KNOWN*** the Father or Me." (John 16:2-3)

A PROPHET IS NOT WELCOME IN THEIR OWN COUNTRY

We talked about the Samaritan woman at the well, in John 4, above, where, "Jesus Himself testified that a ***prophet*** has ***no honor*** in his own country."

Likewise, in Luke 4:24-28,

"Jesus said, 'Truly I say to you, ***no prophet*** is ***welcome*** in his hometown.

But I say to you in truth, there were many widows in Israel in the days of Elijah, when the sky was shut up for three years and six months, when a great famine came over all the land; and yet Elijah was sent to none of them, but only to Zarephath, in the land of Sidon, to a woman who was a widow.

And there were many lepers in Israel in the time of Elisha the prophet; and none of them was cleansed, but only Naaman the Syrian.'

And *ALL* the people in the synagogue were filled with rage as they heard these things."

PROJECTING AND PROPAGANDA

Continuing on from the sections on *"PROJECTION"* and *"THOSE WHO YELL THE LOUDEST"*, above, ninety-nine out of the one hundred *"accusing"* others of *"wrongdoings"* are actually projecting who they are on us.

A note for *"Projecting"*, as well as, *"Propaganda"* [tools used by many]. If you repeat a lie long enough, over and over and over—people will eventually believe it's the truth. The devil does this. So does the world. We see it all the time in politics and the media.

Therefore, it's not surprising in the least that *false leaders,* backed by their spirit rulers, ingrain their false teachings into their Stockholm converts by Repeat and Rote.

Let's see how they play this game on their Stockholm trainees. They may do it with several tactics.

First By Confusion

Remember chocolate?

First, the experts told us, "We studied the effects of chocolate and it's bad for you." Then later they told us, "We studied the effects of chocolate and it's good for you."

Which was it?

They did the same with honey.

Once again, the experts told us, "We studied the effects of honey and it's bad for you." Then later told us, "We studied the effects of honey and it's good for you."

Again, which was it?

They did the same with eggs.

And, again, the experts told us, "We studied the effects of eggs and they're bad for you." Then later told us, "We studied the effects of eggs and they're good for you."

Once again, which was it?

Are you confused yet?

Good!

Then their plan worked!

Second By Indoctrination

After setting you up by confusion, *softening you so you don't resist any longer,* then they indoctrinate you by telling straight up lies.

Such as, "The sky is purple with green streaks and pink polka dots."

Then, when someone questions that statement, it's followed up with a condemning statement, "If you can't see it, then you need help because your spiritual eyes don't work."

Here leaders and other Stockholm *"believers"* will continue to shame these new converts. This shaming will continue to happen until those new converts force themselves to believe what they're being told.

Eventually, they will *"start to see it"*—which will progress into *"finally"* being able to see all the time—with their *NEW spiritual eyes.* Exclaiming, "Oh you are right, the sky is purple with green streaks and pink polka dots. Now I see it."

The constant repetition of such things, without the possibility of introducing common sense or contradiction, eventually convinces people of their *TRUTH,* giving them what they believe are now *NEW* "spiritual eyes." It becomes part of their *NEW Belief System.*

And now, they'll love their [newly fermented] acceptance into an *Elite Group,* an *Elite Club.* So, they too, can also be called *"spiritual",* having *"spiritual eyes".* They'll love that they're now someone who has achieved something *"SPECIAL"* that other "regular" 'ol Believers don't have.

Oh, how they played on their need for acceptance.

Oh, how they played on their egos.

Now part of an Elite Group having New 'spiritual eyes'

CHAPTER TWELVE

TAKE MY YOKE UPON YOU

YOKES CAN BE BAD OR GOOD

WHAT'S A YOKE?

As a Noun, it can mean:

1. A wooden bar or frame by which two draft animals (such as oxen) are joined at the heads or necks for working together.

2. An arched device formerly laid on the neck of a defeated person.

3. A frame fitted to a person's shoulders to carry a load in two equal portions.

4. A frame from which a bell is hung.

5. A clamp or similar piece that embraces two parts to hold or unite them in position.

6. "Yoked": Two animals yoked or worked together.

7. An oppressive agency.

8. Servitude, bondage.

9. A tie, link, such as in marriage.

As a Verb, it can mean:

1. Yoked; yoking.

2. To put a yoke on.

3. To join in or with a yoke.

4. To attach a draft animal to; also, to attach (a draft animal) to something.

5. To join as if by a yoke.

6. To put to work.

7. To become joined or linked.

[as quoted from the Merriam Webster Dictionary® online]

BAD YOKES

Let's pull some definitions from above that define Bad Yokes.

1. An arched device formerly laid on the neck of a *defeated person*.

2. An *oppressive agency*.

3. *Servitude, bondage*.

4. A *tie, link*, such as in marriage.

5. To put a yoke on.

6. To join in or with a yoke.

7. To attach a draft animal to; also, to attach (a draft animal) to something.

8. To join as if by a yoke.

9. To put to work.

10. To become joined or linked.

BAD YOKES are *"an oppressive agency"*, someone or something that *"puts a yoke on"* you, forces you to *"join as if by a yoke"*, forces you to *"be attached like a draft animal* to; also, attaching (a draft animal) to something", and forcing us, *"putting to work"*, for something **NOT** good;

And when they're "laid on the neck of a *defeated person"*, forcing *"servitude, bondage"*, and causing "a *tie, link* [remember curse-links?], such as in *marriage"*, as in married into *false Belief Systems,* they take and keep us **CAPTIVE**.

Men's Yokes

We've talked a lot about the **YOKES** that men [or women] can put on us. **YOKES** put on us by joining into *false Belief Systems,* by becoming *Stockholm converts* and *devotees.*

Demon Yokes

Demon **YOKES** are identical to men's **YOKES**. Because men [or women] didn't come up with their **YOKE** designs by themselves, they learned them from their demon rulers.

Yokes of This World

Once again, the *god* of this world, who has deceived the world since its beginning, has perpetrated these yokes upon us.

Yokes We Put on Ourselves

Again, these **YOKES** have been enacted on us by the *god* of this world who taught us to *ALWAYS* run his mazes.

GOOD YOKES

There's only *ONE*. Jesus.

A good **YOKE** is "a wooden bar or frame by which *two draft animals* (such as oxen) are joined at the heads or necks *for working together*", "a frame fitted to a person's shoulders to *carry* a load in *two equal portions*", "a clamp or similar piece that embraces two parts to hold or unite them in position", *"two animals yoked* or *worked together*", *"a tie, link, such as in marriage* [like the marriage of the Lamb]", "to join in or with a yoke", "to attach a draft animal to; also, to attach (a draft animal) to something", and *"to put to work"*.

Picture two oxen in a yoke, pulling a plow or a wagon together. One of them is massive and much stronger (representing Jesus). The other is much smaller and weaker (representing us). Yet when they pull the load, the stronger one doesn't out power or outpull the weaker. They walk, pull, and work *evenly*—in complete *unison*—in complete *harmony*.

Why?

By design, a **YOKE** can be *adjusted* so that stronger and weaker oxen *pull equally* and in *unison*.

This is how we're to be **YOKED** to Jesus. This is how we're to walk in Him and with Him—*equally* **YOKED**—which is achieved by the Holy Spirit's *transformative adjustments* within us.

Take "My Yoke Upon You"

In Matthew 11:28-30 we see,

"Come to Me, all who are weary and heavy-laden, and I will give you rest.

Take **My YOKE** upon you and learn from Me, for I am gentle and humble in heart, and YOU WILL FIND REST FOR YOUR SOULS.

For **My YOKE** is easy and **My Burden** is light."

In First Corinthians 6:17 it says,

"But the one who **JOINS** himself to the Lord is **ONE Spirit** with Him."

In John 17:21-23,

"That they may all be **ONE**; even as You, Father, are in Me and I in You, that **they** also may be in **Us**, so that the world may believe that You sent Me.

The glory which You have given Me I have given to them, that they may be **ONE**, just as We are **ONE**;

I in **them** and **You** in **Me**, that they may be **Perfected** in **Unity**, so that the world may know that You sent Me, and loved them, even as You have loved Me."

Notice The Difference

Can you see the difference between being *YOKED with Jesus* versus the **BAD YOKES**, above?

BAD YOKES are there to enslave you. To defeat you. To force you to do their biddings.

To be **YOKED** *with Jesus* is to find **Freedom** and **Life** with the **Father**!

OH, WHAT A DIFFERENCE!

BREAK THE YOKES

We're told in Leviticus 26:13,

"I am the LORD your God, who brought you out of the land of **Egypt** so that you would not be their **SLAVES**, and I broke the bars of your **YOKE** and made you walk erect."

And in Deuteronomy 6:21,

"Then you shall say to your son, 'We were **SLAVES** to Pharaoh in **Egypt**, and the LORD brought us from **Egypt** with a mighty hand.'"

Again, in Exodus 6:5-7,

"Furthermore, I have heard the groaning of the sons of Israel, because the Egyptians are holding them in **Bondage** [by **Burdens** and **YOKES**], and I have remembered My covenant.

Say, therefore, to the sons of Israel, 'I am the LORD, and I will bring you out from under the **Burdens** [**Bondage** and **YOKES**] of the Egyptians, and I will deliver you from their **Burdens** [**Bondage** and **YOKES**]. I will also redeem you with an outstretched arm and with great judgments.

Then I will take you for My people, and I will be your God; and you shall know that I am the LORD your God, who brought you out from under the **Burdens** [**Bondage** and **YOKES**] of the Egyptians."

Again, in Deuteronomy 28:47-48,

"Because you did not serve the LORD your God with joy and a glad heart, for the abundance of all things; therefore, you shall serve your enemies whom the LORD will send against you, in hunger, in thirst, in nakedness, and in the lack of all things; and He will put an **Iron YOKE** on your neck until He has destroyed you."

We Know The Bad Yokes

People have put them on themselves.

Men and women have put them on us.

Demons have put them on us.

Churches where demons-in-nations rule have put them on us.

False leaders have put them on us.

False Christs, the spirit of the antichrist, spirit rulers, and the wrong voices have put them on us.

These **YOKES**, all backed by the rulers of this world—by the power of the air.

These **YOKES** tie us to the ruler of this world to keep us in **BONDAGE**.

BEWARE OF FALSE PROPHECIES FROM FALSE PROPHETS

In Jeremiah 28:1-17,

"Now in the same year, in the beginning of the reign of Zedekiah king of Judah, in the fourth year, in the fifth month, Hananiah the son of Azzur, the prophet, who was from Gibeon, spoke to me in the house of the LORD in the presence of the priests and all the people, saying,

'Thus says the LORD of hosts, the God of Israel, "I have broken the **YOKE** of the king of Babylon.

Within two years I am going to bring back to this place all the vessels of the LORD's house, which Nebuchadnezzar king of Babylon took away from this place and carried to Babylon.

I am also going to bring back to this place Jeconiah the son of Jehoiakim, king of Judah, and all the exiles of Judah who went to Babylon," declares the LORD, "for I will break the **YOKE** of the king of Babylon.'"

Then the prophet Jeremiah spoke to the prophet Hananiah in the presence of the priests and in the presence of all the people who were standing in the house of the LORD,

And the prophet Jeremiah said, 'Amen! May the LORD do so; may the LORD confirm your words which you have prophesied to bring back the vessels of the LORD's house and all the exiles, from Babylon to this place.

Yet hear now this word which I am about to speak in your hearing and in the hearing of all the people!

The prophets who were before me and before you from ancient times prophesied against many lands and against great kingdoms, of war and of calamity and of pestilence.

The prophet who prophesies of peace, when the word of the prophet comes to pass, then that prophet will be known as one whom the LORD has truly sent.'

Then Hananiah the prophet took the **YOKE** from the neck of Jeremiah the prophet and **broke it**.

Hananiah spoke in the presence of all the people, saying, 'Thus says the LORD, "Even so will I break within two full years the **YOKE** of Nebuchadnezzar king of Babylon from the neck of all the nations."'

Then the prophet Jeremiah went his way.

The word of the LORD came to Jeremiah after Hananiah the prophet had broken the **YOKE** from off the neck of the prophet Jeremiah, saying,

'Go and speak to Hananiah, saying, "Thus says the LORD, 'You have broken the **YOKES** of **Wood**, but you have made instead of them **YOKES** of *Iron*.

For thus says the LORD of hosts, the God of Israel, 'I have put a *YOKE* of *Iron* on the neck of all these nations, that they may serve Nebuchadnezzar king of Babylon; and they *will Serve* [be *Slaves* to] him. And I have also given him the beasts of the field.'"'

Then Jeremiah the prophet said to Hananiah the prophet, 'Listen now, Hananiah, *THE LORD* has *NOT SENT YOU*, and *YOU HAVE MADE* this *PEOPLE TRUST* in a *LIE*.

Therefore, thus says the LORD, "Behold, I am about to remove you from the face of the earth. This year you are going to die, because you have counseled rebellion against the LORD."'

So Hananiah the prophet died in the same year in the seventh month."

Hananiah's prophesy sounded *SO GOOD,* in the beginning; even Jeremiah thought so [in his own hearing and personal insight]; until the Lord intervened and said otherwise. Then Jeremiah delivered him the bad news while setting the record straight for Israel.

Therefore, take heed: We cannot choose the prophecies we prefer or the prophets we want to listen to. We've continued to discuss *false prophets* based on *false anointings* in this book and the last. Both clearly define how God's leaders can start out operating from a good place with His gifts, but are able to misuse them later. Because *"God's gifts and callings are irrevocable"*.

Be sure the demon rulers over the kingdoms of religions and denominations will hold God's people *CAPTIVE* with *false prophesies* from *false prophets*.

THIS YOKE WILL KEEP US FREE!

After our liberation, many of us will still not choose to walk with the Father, living a life by the Spirit of God, and will unfortunately demand new leaders, just as Israel did.

Setting God's people free was and is **NOT** to go from one **BONDAGE** to the next.

"It was for **FREEDOM** that **Christ [the Anointing] Set Us Free;** therefore, keep standing firm and do not be **Subject** again to a **YOKE** of **Slavery.**" (Galatians 5:1)

CHAPTER THIRTEEN

THE [F—ED UP] MIXTURE IN US

WE ARE ALL A F—ED UP MIXTURE

E VERYONE HAS *Unholy Mixtures* inside us—*YES*, I mean *ALL* of us—including me. None of us can escape this categorization—*NONE—except Jesus.*

And, if you claim to be Him "reincarnated" or Him returning in or through you, then you have a lot bigger problems than just being a F—ed up mixture. More like being *TOTALLY* deceived and ruled by the spirit of the antichrist.

Even if you don't claim to be the new "return of Christ", but somehow think you're not a F—ed up mixture; because you're "too spiritual" or "too holy"; you're still *"HIGH"* or *"DRUNK"*, sucking on your own *"EGO JUICE"*; and under the spell of the *god* of this world.

HEARING MANY VOICES

We talked previously [in this book and the first] about hearing the many, many voices that come to us. All of them wrong, except from the True and Living God. Proven only by His Word and His Peace that passes understanding.

These voices started out [as noted] from the ruler of this world. But the INDOCTRINATION of God's people has amplified them in the churches by *false leaders* under their demon rulers.

WHERE ARE THE F—ED UP MIXTURES?

In us.

In the churches.

In the world.

In our hearts.

In our minds.

In our beliefs.

Everywhere.

CAN ANY OF US BE FREE?

YES.

But it's part of the *lifelong Sanctification process* God is doing in us—**if**, and **only if**, we are willing.

Hence, we **MUST** learn to **Choose**, **Yield**, and **Believe** to allow His process to work in us each day.

UNDERSTANDING IT'S A LIFELONG PROCESS

Again, receiving His word to us,

"It was for **FREEDOM** that **Christ** *[the **Anointing**]* **Set Us Free;** therefore, keep standing firm and do not be **Subject** again to a **YOKE** of **Slavery.**"

And,

"Therefore, there is now **No Condemnation** for those who are In **CHRIST** *[the **Anointing**]* Jesus, because through **CHRIST** *[the Anointing]* Jesus, the law of the *[**HOLY**] **SPIRIT** [the **Anointing**]* who gives life, **Has Set You Free.**" (Romans 8:1–2)

Therefore, let's NOT get under condemnation again.

That's just another waste of time deception by the ruler of this world. Choose not to waste your precious time in that depressing place. Or he wins again.

Remember: It's a Choice.

Achieving such is only possible through moment by moment Yielding.

And Believing.

CHAPTER FOURTEEN

IT'S NOT BASED ON PERFECTION

BE PERFECT AS I AM PERFECT

AS WE MENTIONED PREVIOUSLY, but needs to be emphasized again, we need to get something straight now and forever [for as long as we are living on the earth]—it's not about being *"Perfect"*—none of us can **EVER** be *"Perfect."* There was and is only one who was **EVER Perfect** on earth and that was Jesus, alone.

There's NO perfection in us [of ourselves].

There's NONE in the churches.

There's NONE in Belief Systems.

There's NONE in anything.

Again, you might want to argue that statement by quoting Matthew 5:48, where Jesus told us,

"Therefore, you are to be *Perfect*, as your heavenly Father is *Perfect.*"

Since Jesus told us to be *Perfect*, then it sure sounds like it *MUST* be possible. Therefore, there *MUST* be a way that we can somehow live a *"Perfect"* life.

Again, looking deeper. Matthew 5:48 in the AMP version reads:

"You, therefore, must be *Perfect* [growing into *complete maturity* of *godliness* in *mind* and *character*, having reached the proper height of virtue and integrity], as your heavenly Father is *Perfect.*"

Remember the word *Perfect* in the Greek is 'teleios' (TEH-lei-os), meaning *"having reached its end," "i.e., 'complete', by extension, 'perfect',"* *"mature," "more perfect,"* from the root word 'telos' (TEH-los) which means *"an end," "continually," "[until it's] finished," "[until it's reached its intended] fulfillment," "[until it's reached its intended] goal," "[until it's reached its intended] outcome."*

This kind of *Perfection* is the exact same process as *Sanctification* we discussed above. It's a lifelong process—here on earth—never ending; until it's reached its intended *"fulfillment," "goal," "outcome,"* and *"end."* Remember, "the earth is a testing ground."

Again in Philippians 3:12-15 we're told,

"NOT that I have now *attained* [this ideal], or have already been made *PERFECT*, but I press on to *lay hold* of *(grasp)* and *make my own*, that for which *Christ [the Anointing]* Jesus has laid hold of me and made me His own.

I do not consider, brethren, that I have captured and made it my own [*yet*]; but one thing I do [it is my one aspiration]: *forgetting* what lies *behind* and *straining forward* to what lies *ahead*,

I press on toward the goal to win the [supreme and heavenly] prize to which God in *Christ [the Anointing]* Jesus is calling us upward.

So let those [of us] who are *spiritually mature* and *full-grown* have this mind and hold these convictions; and if in any respect you have a different attitude of mind, God will make that clear to you also."

Hence, let's garner this same mind—it's about *Seeking, Yielding, Believing,* and *Walking* with the Lord [or allowing Him to walk with us] throughout this life. Let us learn to *Focus* on *Him* versus our lack of perfection. So that we can live in *His Presence, His Anointing*, and *His Peace*.

Because when we're *NEAR* the Father, the Lord, and the Holy Spirit, we are in the *Presence* of *Perfection*. Thereby, we become *PERFECT* in those moments!

Live for those moments!

As a deer pants after water, strive after the Lord for many more!

REMEMBER: DON'T BE RELIGIOUS

Don't try to fake out yourself, others, or God.

Be real.

Be honest.

Love the Truth.

We can *NEVER* be perfect enough. We can *NEVER* be good enough. It's by Grace we've been saved, not on our own or anything by our righteousness—at best, we are unworthy servants. We can use the *ONLY* powers we've been given: *CHOICE* and *YIELDING*.

Remembering the secret repeated over and over in the first book:

"We're a vessel to whomever we yield."

Since you can never be good enough on your own—stop trying—start yielding.

THE "WORK" NEEDS TO BE PERFECT

Now you say, "What!"

"After just telling us that we can **NEVER** be **Perfect**, you now tell us we are to be **Perfect** again."

"What's up with that?"

We'll visit one more piece to the **Perfection Puzzle** after we discuss "THIS IS THE WORK OF GOD" in the upcoming chapter, "HOW TO STAY FREE".

CHAPTER FIFTEEN

I ONLY WANT TO HEAR YOU

NOTHING ELSE

I LOVE CODY CARNES' SONG "NOTHING ELSE"

L ET'S LOOK AT HIS lyrics.

[Chorus]
I'm caught up in Your presence
I just want to sit here at Your feet
I'm caught up in this holy moment
I never want to leave
And oh, I'm not here for blessings
Jesus, You don't owe me anything
More than anything that You can do
Oh, I just want You

[Verse 1]
I'm sorry when I've just gone through the motions
I'm sorry when I just sang another song

Take me back to where we started
I open up my heart to You

[Verse 2]
I'm sorry when I've come with my agenda
I'm sorry when I forgot that You're enough
Take me back to where we started
I open up my heart to You

[Chorus]
I'm caught up in Your presence
I just want to sit here at Your feet
I'm caught up in this holy moment
I never want to leave
And oh, I'm not here for blessings
Jesus, You don't owe me anything
More than anything that You can do
Oh, I just want You

[Bridge]
I just want You
Nothing else, nothing else
Nothing else will do
I just want You
Nothing else, nothing else
Nothing else will do
I just want You
Nothing else, nothing else
Nothing else will do
I just want You
Nothing else, nothing else, Jesus
Nothing else will do
I just want You
Nothing else, nothing else
Nothing else will do

I just want You
Nothing else, nothing else, Jesus
Nothing else will do

[Spontaneous]
I'm coming back to where we started
I'm coming back to where we started
When I first felt Your love
You're all that matters, Jesus
You're all that matters
I'm coming back to what really matters
Just Your heart
I just want to bless Your heart, Jesus

[Chorus]
I'm caught up in Your presence
I just want to sit here at Your feet
I'm caught up in this holy moment
I never want to leave
And oh, I'm not here for blessings
Jesus, You don't owe me anything
More than anything that You can do
Oh, I just want You

[Copyright by Cody Carnes; from his Album: "Run To The Father"]

Cody said it really well in this song. He realized he began the right way in the Presence of the Father—then over time—he lost sight. This happens too many, many others. I know it's happened to me.

Cody tells us in his song how when he realized his mistakes; where he got "caught up" doing "good things" [creating songs for God's people] he lost sight of his original purpose; and the original place of being in and living out of the Presence of the Father.

He also addresses the deception we all face when we come to the Lord with our "agenda" and forgot the Lord had *ALWAYS* been enough.

SET THE CAPTIVES FREE

Let's *ALL* come back to this *Simple Place* of seeking the Lord for Himself and "NOTHING ELSE."

TAKING ALL THOUGHTS CAPTIVE

FROM THE FOREWORD IN THE FIRST BOOK

"For though we walk (live) in the flesh, we are not carrying on our warfare according to the flesh and using mere human weapons. For the weapons of our warfare are not physical [weapons of flesh and blood], but they are mighty before God for the overthrow and destruction of strongholds (or fortresses), [inasmuch as we] refute arguments, theories, speculations, reasonings, vain imaginations, and every proud, high, and lofty thing (or thought) that sets itself up against the [true] knowledge of God; and we lead every thought and purpose away *captive* into the *obedience* of *Christ.* "(2 Corinthians 10:3–5 AMP)

We see the end result is for us to take all these thoughts and purposes [arguments, theories, speculations, reasonings, vain imaginations, and every proud, high, and lofty thing (or thought); that sets itself up against the [true] knowledge of God]; *CAPTIVE* into the *Obedience* of *Christ*.

First, unlike *Belief Systems*, it's important to note this is a *Captivity* in *Christ* where we are to be *YOKED* to Him and live in.

Let's take a quick minute to define what that really means practically for us in our daily lives.

Remember what we mentioned previously and the full chapter in the first book explaining *Christ* is *NOT* Jesus's last name. It means *the Anointing*. And we're to live in and out of *Christ [the Anointing]*. Please reread that chapter if you still have questions on this subject.

Then the only question remains, "What's the **Obedience** that we're to do in *the* **Anointing?**"

The **Obedience** *is* **Yielding**.

Do you remember all we've discussed so far and in both books about **Yielding**? If not, it's way too important, so please go back and review. There you'd see, again, that **Choice** and **Yielding** are the *ONLY* powers we have in the spiritual realm.

Therefore, to **Obey** *the* **Anointing** is to **YIELD** ourselves to the **Holy Spirit** to allow *the* **Anointing** to flow in and through us. Hence, when we take these thoughts and purposes [arguments, theories, speculations, reasonings, vain imaginations, and every proud, high, and lofty thing (or thought) that sets itself up against the (true) knowledge of God] **Captive** into the **Yielding** of *the* **Anointing**, we can be set free from **ALL Bondages** and **other Captivities**. All part of our **DAILY STAND**.

"HOT POTATO"

Taking our *thoughts* **Captive** is, again, another game of "Hot Potato". Where we *ACTIVELY* "cast", "pass", and "take" **EVERY** thought **Captive**, by **Yielding** to the Holy Spirit.

ALL OTHER VOICES BE STILL!

WITH SINGULAR PURPOSE

We need to set our hearts, minds, and face to this singular purpose: We only want to hear from the Father, the Lord Jesus, the Holy Spirit, and His angels.

When we learn ***THE DAILY STAND***, we will know how to do this.

And we'll learn how to tell all the other voices, ***"Be Still!"***

CHAPTER SIXTEEN

SUFFICIENT TO THE MOMENT IS THE EVIL [or TROUBLE] THEREIN

WHY THE DAILY STAND?

KEEPING WATCH

Do remember in the first book where we discussed, "Why the Daily Stand?"

Where in Matthew 6:34 (AMP) we were told,

"So do not worry or be anxious about tomorrow, for tomorrow will have worries and anxieties of its own. Sufficient for each day is its own trouble."

And in the King James Version, where it says,

"Take therefore no thought for the morrow: for the morrow shall take thought for the things of itself. Sufficient unto the day is the evil thereof (or there in)."

Where I noted, I like to take this verse one step further.

"Sufficient unto the **MOMENT** is the evil [or trouble] thereof (or there in)."

We need to recognize that the enemy does *NOT* take a day off or a moment off—therefore, neither should we.

Not only in seeking the Father.

Not only in Praying.

Not only in Standing.

But ALSO in Keeping Watch.

For all the schemes of the devil to undermine our lives, the Church [the true Body of Christ], and our *healthy Beliefs* in the *healthy, true,* and *pure doctrine* [teachings] of the Word.

NOT the *false doctrines* of men or demons [as discussed earlier in "BELIEF SYSTEMS ~ THE STOCKHOLM SYNDROME"].

IF IT WAS UP TO US

BY OUR CAPABILITIES

We could never do this,

EVER.

But if we live in the Spirit and out of the Presence of God,

We can.

CHAPTER SEVENTEEN

TIME TO TURN THE CORNER

TAKE THE CALL

A DISPENSATION OF THE SPIRIT

G OD GIVES OPPORTUNITIES ONCE in a while. A time I like to call *a dispensation of the Spirit.* Where the Holy Spirit is tugging at your heart and mind, asking you if you'll listen to the Father.

Take the call when he knocks.

We love to quote Revelation 3:20 when leading people to the Lord,

"Behold, I stand at the door and knock; if anyone hears My voice and opens the door, I will come in to him and will dine with him, and he with Me."

But did you know that's not really the context and what this verse means?

It was actually a message to one of the seven churches in the book of Revelations. These churches were to receive their report card—good or bad—with praise and/or correction. These same messages are a type for us to learn the same in the churches today.

In Revelation 3:14-22 it says,

"To the angel of the church in Laodicea write: The Amen, the faithful and true Witness, the Beginning of the creation of God, says this:

'I know your deeds, that you are neither cold nor hot; I wish that you were cold or hot. So because you are lukewarm, and neither hot nor cold, I will spit you out of My mouth.

Because you say, "I am rich, and have become wealthy, and have need of nothing," and you do not know that you are wretched and miserable and poor and blind and naked,

I advise you to buy from Me gold refined by fire so that you may become rich, and white garments so that you may clothe yourself, and that the shame of your nakedness will not be revealed; and eye salve to anoint your eyes so that you may see.

Those whom I *love*, I *reprove* and *discipline;* therefore, be *zealous* and *repent*.

[now] Behold, I stand at the door and knock; if anyone hears My voice and opens the door, I will come in to him and will dine with him, and he with Me.

He who overcomes, I will grant to him to sit down with Me on My throne, as I also overcame and sat down with My Father on His throne.

He who has an ear, let him hear what the Spirit says to the churches.'"

Therefore, verse twenty's context centers on a rebuke of the church that once panted and sought after the Lord; but now has become complacent and lukewarm. Here the Lord is counseling them, "Buy from Me gold refined by fire so that you may become *rich* [in Me], and *white garments* so that you may *clothe yourself* [in My purity]... and *eye salve* to *anoint* your *eyes* so that you may *see*", then, "*Pay attention* when I come to the *door* [of your heart] and *knock*", and if you do, "*I will come in* and *dine with you* [have *intimate fellowship* with you]."

209

The Lord was speaking to Believers here—not unbelievers.

[Sorry for those who think this verse is for trying to convert the latter.]

These are the opportunities, once in a while, the **dispensation** of the **Spirit**, where the Holy Spirit is tugging at your heart and mind, *asking* you if you'll **listen** to the **Father**.

TAKE THE CALL

OR GO IN TO THE WILDERNESS

YOUR CHOICE

If you don't take the call, you're indirectly choosing to go into the wilderness. And probably for a longer time and a longer route than you might've had to go through otherwise.

Remember Jesus saying,

"WHOEVER is NOT WITH ME is AGAINST ME, and whoever does not gather with me scatters." (Luke 11:23)

There's no middle ground. You can't have it your own way. This isn't Burger King®.

So, will you choose to go through the storms to wait to see if He gives you another call and another chance?

I sincerely hope He does.

He is gracious.

He may call a second time.

He may call a third time.

But I'd advise you, "To **buy** from Me ***gold refined*** by ***fire***", the next time He asks.

CHAPTER EIGHTEEN

QUESTIONS TO ASK YOURSELF

HOW MANY KNOW THEY'RE IN CAPTIVITY?

M OST LIKELY, THOSE WHO are in *Captivity* do not.

DO PEOPLE EVEN RECOGNIZE WHAT CAPTIVITY IS?

Again, most likely those who are in *Captivity* do not.

DO THEY EVEN CARE IF

THEY ARE?

Sadly, they probably don't.

Unless they're open enough to let themselves feel the sadness, pain, and anguish from time to time throughout their lives.

DO YOU KNOW IF YOU ARE?

ONLY if you're open to the Holy Spirit's tugging.

And being willing to hear the Lord knocking at your heart.

If so, Please Answer.

A GOOD TEST

FIRST QUESTION:

Do you *love* your religion or denomination *more* than the *Lord Himself*?

I'm hoping most would answer, *"NO."*

SECOND QUESTION:

Could you *EASILY* and *IMMEDIATELY* walk away from your religion or denomination?

Being willing to go into the wilderness.

If the *Lord* asked you to do that to be *Set Free*.

THE SECOND QUESTION IS THE REAL TEST

It determines if you've become a *Stockholm devotee.*

And how deeply you've been engrained in to *false Belief Systems.*

EXAMINE, TEST, AND EVALUATE

Second Corinthians 13:5 tells us,

"*EXAMINE* and *TEST* and *EVALUATE* your own selves to see whether you are *Holding* to your *Faith* and *Showing* the *PROPER FRUITS* of it. *TEST* and *PROVE* yourselves (not Christ). Do you not yourselves *Realize* and *Know* [thoroughly by an ever-increasing experience] that Jesus *Christ [the Anointing]* is in you;

Unless you are *[COUNTERFEITS] Disapproved* on *Trial* and *Rejected?*"

You must understand the critical, even spiritually life-or-death importance of these *QUESTIONS* and this *TEST*.

They will determine if it's *Christ [the Anointing]* the Hope of Glory (Colossians 1:25–27) being formed in you, or *COUNTERFEITS*, with no hope.

THEREFORE, DO NOT IGNORE THEM!

CHAPTER NINETEEN

SET THE CAPTIVES FREE

LOSING PART OF OUR SOUL

H AVE YOU EVER HEARD the old sayings, "That this person [or thing] now occupies your mind.", "They now own a piece of your soul.", and "You're letting them [or giving them permission to] take up residence in your mind."?

Unfortunately, these sayings are true.

Remember Dick's niece? I allowed this shameful incident to take ownership of a piece of my mind and *hold me Captive* for many years.

Remember Dick's twelve-year-old nephew? Again, I allowed this sad incident *to* take ownership of a piece of my mind and *hold me Captive* for many years.

Unless we allow God to do this work in us—to change us—from the inside out; then we're doomed to live a life *way below the potential* we have in Him or *WORSE*.

Guaranteed: If we don't get out from under all these ***Captivities***, then "losing our minds" might be the least that can happen to us.

Therefore, submit yourself to God in *ALL* these areas, willing to come out of Egypt, and go into the wilderness without trying to build "new gods" during your time there. Allowing Him to complete His process in you *FULLY* so you can truly be free in Him.

I HAVE COME TO SET THE CAPTIVES FREE

As stated in the Forward, but now seen from the AMP version, Jesus said in Luke 4:18-19,

"The Spirit of the Lord [is] upon Me, because He has anointed Me [the ***Anointed One***, the Messiah] to preach the ***Good News*** (the Gospel) to the poor; He has sent Me to ***ANNOUNCE RELEASE*** to the ***CAPTIVES*** and ***RECOVERY*** of ***SIGHT*** to the ***BLIND***, to send forth as ***DELIVERED THOSE WHO*** are ***OPPRESSED*** [who are downtrodden, bruised, crushed, and broken down by calamity] [to ***SET*** the ***OPPRESSED*** [***CAPTIVES***] ***FREE***]

To proclaim the accepted and acceptable year of the Lord [the ***Day*** when ***Salvation*** and the ***Free Favors*** of ***God Profusely Abound***.]"

And Jesus was quoting this from Isaiah 61:1 where it says,

"The Spirit of the Lord God is upon me, because the Lord has anointed and qualified me to proclaim ***Good News*** to the poor [to preach the Gospel of good tidings to the meek, the poor, and afflicted]; He has sent me to ***BIND UP*** and ***HEAL*** the ***BROKENHEARTED***, to ***PROCLAIM LIBERTY [FREEDOM]*** to the [***PHYSICAL*** and ***SPIRITUAL] CAPTIVES*** and the ***OPENING*** of the ***PRISON*** and of the ***EYES*** to ***THOSE*** who are ***BOUND*** [and ***RELEASE*** from ***DARKNESS*** for the ***PRISONERS***]."

Jesus Came to Set Us FREE!

That was His mission and goal. And He paid the ultimate price for us and our freedom.

But did He do this just for our salvation from hell, so we can go to Heaven?

Which should be enough.

NO.

He did it for every part of our lives, from that initial moment of salvation [when we asked the Lord into our life] throughout every area of our life. For every minute of every day. For us to be *SET FREE* from *ALL* that would entangle us.

God knows *ALL* the challenges that will come our direction—all the time—in every way. He knows we need the continuous work of the Holy Spirit in us to *Set* and *Keep Us Free*.

HERE'S HOW MUCH HE CARES FOR US

Again, from Galatians 5:1 it says,

"It was for *FREEDOM* that *Christ [the Anointing] Set Us Free;* therefore, keep standing firm and do not be *Subject* again to a *YOKE* of *Slavery*."

And in John 8:31–32,

"So Jesus said, 'if you *CONTINUE* in My word, then you are truly disciples of Mine; and you will *Know* the *Truth*, and the *Truth* will make you *free*.'"

In John 14:6,

"Jesus said, 'I AM the Way and the Truth and the Life; no one comes to the Father except by [through] Me.'"

And again from Romans 8:1–2 it says,

"Therefore, there is now no condemnation for those who are In **CHRIST** *[the **Anointing**]* Jesus, because through **CHRIST** *[the **Anointing**]* Jesus, the law of the *[HOLY] SPIRIT [the **Anointing**]* who gives life, **HAS SET YOU FREE**."

In Psalms 102:19-20 it says,

"For He looked down from His holy height;

From Heaven the LORD gazed upon the earth,

To hear the groaning of the prisoner,

To **SET FREE** those who were **doomed** to **death**."

In Hosea 11:1-4, God yearns over His people,

"When Israel was a youth **I loved him**, and out of **Egypt I called** My son.

The more they called them, the more they went from them;

They kept sacrificing to the Baals and burning incense to idols.

Yet it is **I who taught** Ephraim [meaning "fruitful"—reflecting the blessings his people received] **to walk**,

I took them in **My arms**;

But they did not **Know** that **I Healed** them.

I led them with cords of a man, with **Bonds** of **Love**,

And **I became to them** as one who lifts the **Yoke** from their jaws;

And **I bent down** and **Fed** them."

In Zechariah 9:11 it says,

"As for you also, **because** of the **Blood** of **My Covenant** with you, I have **Set** your **Prisoners Free** from the **waterless pit**."

SHOUT FOR JOY AND REJOICE

In Isaiah 49:8-13 it says,

"Thus says the LORD, 'In a *Favorable Time* I have *Answered* You, and in a day of *Salvation* I have *Helped* You; and I will keep You and give You for a covenant of the people, to *Restore* the *Land* [the Heart], to make them *Inherit* the desolate heritages;

Saying to those who are *Bound*, *"Go forth,"* to those who are in *Darkness*, *"Show Yourselves."* Along the roads they will feed, and their pasture will be on all bare heights.

They will not hunger or thirst, nor will the scorching heat or sun strike them down; For He who has compassion on them will *Lead them* and will *Guide them* to *springs* of *water*.

I will make all My mountains a road, and My highways will be raised up. Behold, these will come from afar; And lo, these will come from the north and from the west, and these from the land of Sinim.'

Shout for *Joy*, O heavens! And *Rejoice*, O earth! *Break forth* into *Joyful shouting*, O mountains! For the LORD has *Comforted His people* and will have *Compassion* on *His afflicted*."

YOU HAVE A CHOICE

In Psalms 146:5-9, we see the faithfulness of God,

"How *BLESSED* is he whose *Help* is the God of Jacob, whose *Hope* is in the LORD his God,

Who made Heaven and earth, the sea and all that is in them;

Who keeps faith forever;

Who executes justice for the *oppressed;*

Who gives food to the *hungry.*

The LORD sets the *prisoners free.*

The LORD opens the *eyes* of the *blind;*

The LORD raises up those who are *bowed down;*

The LORD loves the *righteous;*

The LORD protects the *strangers;*

He supports the *fatherless* and the *widow,*

But He *THWARTS* the *way* of the *wicked."*

Then in Psalms 68:6 we see,

"God makes a home for the lonely;

He *leads out* the *prisoners* into *prosperity,*

Only the *rebellious* [choose to] *dwell* in a *parched land."*

It's Our Choice

It's time to *Humble Ourselves* and *Admit* we're *Prisoners* in *Egypt* and Need Help to be led into Prosperity (*Freedom* from *Captivity*).

Or remain Rebellious and Choose to Dwell [Live] in a Parched Land [Forever?].

I Will Remember My Covenant

God wants us to repent—then He will remember and restore His covenant with us.

In Ezekiel 16:53-54, 60, we see God rebuking Israel, comparing her [as a harlot] to all the surrounding countries.

"Nevertheless, I will **restore** their **Captivity**, the captivity of Sodom and her daughters, the captivity of Samaria and her daughters, and along with them your own **Captivity**,

In order that you may bear your **humiliation** and **feel ashamed** for all that you have done when you become a consolation to them.

Nevertheless, I will remember **My Covenant** with you [from] in the days of **your youth**, and **I will establish** an **Everlasting Covenant** with you."

NOW HE WANTS US TO GO OUT AND DO THE SAME

After we've received this **FREEDOM**, just as Jesus did for us, we're called to share this **FREEDOM** with **ALL** our brethren.

In Isaiah 42:6–8 it says,

"I, the Lord, have called you in (My) righteousness

I will take hold of your hand

I will keep you

And will **make you** to be a **Covenant** for the **people**

And a **Light** for the **gentiles**

To **Open Eyes** that are **Blind**

To **FREE CAPTIVES** from **PRISON**

And to **RELEASE** from the **DUNGEON** those who **Sit** in **Darkness**

I am the Lord; that is My name!

I will not yield My glory to another or My praise to idols."

NOTICE

Unlike the *Stockholm devotees* of *false Belief Systems,*

We're called to **SHARE** this freedom.

Not to impose our wills, the wills of *false leaders,* or the wills of ruler demon-in-nations on the innocents.

CHAPTER TWENTY

HOW TO STAY FREE

ALWAYS COME FROM A PLACE OF HUMILITY

HEARING FROM THE LORD

*A*LL BELIEVERS CAN HEAR from the Lord. We *ALL* can hear His still small voice.

Gifts of The Spirit

The Holy Spirit gives us gifts to help uplift the Church, Believers, and to speak or reach out to unbelievers. We mentioned them earlier from First Corinthians 12.

As stated, God gives gifts to *ALL* His people. Yet again, just because God gives gifts to men and women doesn't mean they're something special or deserve it, as stated in Romans 11,

"For *GOD'S GIFTS*, and *HIS CALL*, are *IRREVOCABLE*.

He never withdraws them when once they are given,

And, He does not change His mind about those to whom He gives His Grace, or to whom He sends His call."

Again, Let's Revisit God's Negative Statement That His Gifts Are Irrevocable

Did He mean that maybe they should be revoked sometimes or many times?

YES.

If it depended upon us and our "good works," they should. Remembering this: never magnify people or gifts. People don't have gifts because they're "special."

They have them because God gave them, and He never took them away no matter what, even if they listened, followed, and functioned out of the wrong (false) anointings.

Therefore, never think too highly of people or their gifts.

Use of Gifts in The Churches

Paul teaches us in Corinthians how we are to operate, in proper order, using the gifts of the Spirit in church gatherings. I will not review this, since that's not the focus here.

But understand Paul spent a lot of time correcting the Corinthians about their misuse of the gifts. Always bear this in mind: people can misuse God's gifts—whether or not part of *false Belief Systems*—remember they're irrevocable by His decree.

A Dim Mirror

Remember when we learned earlier [which will be expanded even more, shortly] that we *ONLY* see in a Mirror dimly? That we *ONLY* hear in part—we *ONLY* see in part—we *ONLY* know in part. We *MUST* always keep that in the forefront of our minds.

Hence, we should ALWAYS come from a place of humility.

When you're tempted to say I heard from the Lord or "Thus says the Lord" be careful—be very careful. As young Christians, as uninformed Christians, as proud [the wrong kind of pride] Christians, as deceived Christians, we're tempted to do this—*BUT DON'T.*

Many times we read in the Old Testament where Ezekiel, Isaiah, Jeremiah, and the other prophets would prophesy that way, always beginning with, "Thus says the Lord." And on those days when we feel some kind of "righteous indignation", we're tempted to repeat the same. Just as we believe the Lord would deliver the message Himself. In the same way, He showed His righteous indignation when He overturned the money-changers' tables in the Temple. Jesus did it—so we think we should too, when we feel the Spirit.

BUT AGAIN, DON'T.

Instead, come from a Humble place saying, "I sense", "I feel", or "I believe" "that the Lord is saying 'this or that.'" Not, "Thus says the Lord... this is the Word of the Lord to you", whether pronouncing "judgements" or even "blessings" [remembering the false prophet that God dealt with by the hand of Jeremiah, we saw previously].

Never assume that you or anyone else is infallible—that mistakes are impossible—that wrong spirits might mislead them; or even that the Lord might test their hearts by letting them receive the wrong message.

LET ME GIVE YOU SOME EXAMPLES

CROSS-COUNTRY TRIP

When I was nineteen, I went on a cross-country trip. I was just about to start college, but felt the Lord wanted me to drive across the US from Columbus, Ohio [where I lived] to Eureka, California [where my brother, Bruce, was living with the Jesus people in those days].

There's a long, long, long involved story about this trip, which I'll cover [in detail] in one of my upcoming books called *MANY MIRACLES*. But for now, I will only discuss this one small piece.

You remember the 'ol "I was poorer than a church mouse" from the first book? Things were much the same for me at this point. I had worked for a full year after graduating high school doing rough construction. It was only occasional work because of the weather and a less than reliable boss. So, I had extremely limited funds for this trip; after I'd paid all my bills, including preliminary entry fees for college.

I was more than willing to hitchhike across the country, but the Lord clearly said, "No, drive." My car drove ok, but I wasn't sure it could make a cross-country trip and back, especially on its four *totally* bald tires. When I said bald, I mean bald. There was *zero* tread left on any of them; there was hardly an image of where the tread had originally been.

After filling the tank of my 'ol '62 Chevy, I only had $3.50 in cash left; without going into all the reasons and details. I will explain that in *MANY MIRACLES*.

Well, the short story [for here] was I ran out of gas on the I-70 Interstate passing midway through the State of Kansas—in the middle of nowhere. I rolled the last few feet on to the right-side berm.

It was about 7 am. I prayed. A lot. And a lot more. "I believe You sent me, so Lord what are You going to do now?"

Then I heard the Lord say, "I'll provide for you by 4 o'clock."

Ok, now I could relax.

Oh, by the way, I didn't own a watch, so I just sat there waiting.

I prayed.

I read my bible.

I sang.

I worshipped.

Just waiting and waiting.

Maybe it was around noon, just guessing by the sun being directly overhead, when a mean, gnarly Kansas State trooper pulled up behind my car. When he found out what I was doing there, driving across the country with *NO* money, he read me the riot act. Actually, my first stop was Denver, so I only told him I was going there—which was half true; I didn't have the guts to tell him the whole story. And, yet, he still yelled a lot.

Now, I felt scared.

He said, "There's a small town about 10 miles up. When I get back, I'll bring you a gallon of gas. And when you get there, you better figure out how to get some money to get some gas to go forward or go home. Because I never want to see you on the side of one of 'my roads' ever again."

Now, I felt DOUBLY scared.

I was no longer happy, singing or worshipping. I began praying fervently, "Please hurry up with Your answer and send me that gas by 4 pm.", "Send a Christian with a gas can and money.", "Or an angel with a gas can and money." I didn't care as long as it was before that cop got back.

I finally relaxed and came back to a peaceful place.

Trusting in the Lord [again].

With no watch or any way to tell time, I just waited, watching the sun slowly go down.

I was sure it had to be past 4 pm.

Then the sun set.

Now it had to be 7 to 8 pm.

Then night and pure darkness came.

Other than the beautiful stars in the sky, I wasn't appreciating much at that moment.

I got depressed.

I no longer had *ANY* joy in anything.

If the same Lord told me to drive my car on this trip, had said He'd send the answer by 4 o'clock, and hadn't, then did I *EVER* hear Him at all?

I was full of doubt.

Fear overcame me.

Then suddenly I realized maybe He'd meant 4 am since He didn't say which 4 o'clock. Oh, that made sense. So now I felt better. I could pray and relax again.

I stayed awake most of the night. Praying. Imagining how it was going to play out. I figured the Lord was going to wake up a Believer who lived close by who would follow the Holy Spirit's direction to bring me a can of gas and some money. I prayed and waited.

When that person didn't show up. I was sure that an angel [since we entertain them unaware (Hebrews 13:2)] was going to come with the gas and money. I prayed and waited.

That didn't happen either.

Eventually I watched the beautiful sunrise—but I couldn't appreciate the beauty. I knew it had to be around 7 am again. I got depressed. Then more time passed, watching the sun rising, and I got even more depressed. And when that wasn't enough, I got triply depressed.

Here I am, stuck out in the middle of Kansas—no way forward—no way back. Hey, maybe I could just abandon my car and all my stuff and hitchhike home. That'd stink, because then I wouldn't have a car anymore to get around, let alone to go to college every day. Oh yeah, then they'd just look up my license plate and come find me, and then fine me, in Ohio.

All these plans sucked.

As the sun rose to high noon, I was numb.

Then the sun started going down, and I was without hope.

This was the worst disaster I'd ever been involved in. And I did it, trusting I'd heard the Lord.

What was I thinking?

About that time, the thing I feared the most—the same mean, gnarly Kansas State trooper pulled up behind my car—*AGAIN.*

I prepared myself for the worst.

I figured I was going to jail.

He bellowed, "What in the hell are you still doing here?"

"You could've walked to that next town, 10 miles away, up and back, multiple times over by now."

I sheepishly replied, "You said to wait here and you'd bring a gallon of gas."

He gruffly responded, "Yeah, I guess I did say that."

At which time, he put one gallon of gas into my tank. I attempted to start the car. It turned over for a bit before the gas reached the engine and then started.

That was the first good thing about this trip.

I stepped out of the car again, as directed by the mean, gnarly trooper; who wanted to continue berating me until I felt like crawling under a rock.

He yelled.

He scolded.

He belittled.

He threatened.

And when that wasn't enough, he started all over and repeated everything again.

He gave me his last parting words, "You go up this next town. You go get some money. I don't care who you call. I don't care how you get it. *But you better do it legally.* Then you get some gas and get on down the road. And, if I *EVER* find you on the side of one of my roads here in Kansas, again, I'll give you a nice warm place to sleep for a long time."

I knew what he meant.

He still needed to say more, "It's Saturday night and that little town closes up by 5 pm. So, you better get going quick."

At 5 pm, I thought? 5 pm?

I said, "One last thing. What time is it?"

He said, "4 o'clock."

IT WAS 4 O'CLOCK!

Just one and a half days later.

After that I learned to ask the Lord, "Which day? Which week? Which month? Which year?" I also learned to *NEVER* assume I heard correctly or fully understood what He said.

230

NOR SHOULD YOU.

This is just the beginning of that story. There's a lot more. If this snippet intrigued you, read the complete story in **MANY MIRACLES**, when it comes out someday.

HURRICANE HELENE

Just this past fall, Hurricane Helene devastated many areas, including where we live in South Carolina. Fortunately, our house, roof, and surroundings had very minor damage. But we lost power around 6 am that morning as we heard tornadic winds surrounding, shaking our house.

I prayed for our and others' safety.

When the winds calmed down, my wife and I assessed the property, and most everything was good, minus power in our house. It was the same for all our closest neighbors.

My wife asked me to pray and ask God when the power and lights would come on. I hate being put into that corner. I'd rather have not asked knowing my past on hearing about times, dates, and places. But as a good husband, I did.

The Lord replied with "Seven."

So, begrudgingly, I told her the news.

She knew about my 4 o'clock on the side of the road story, so she jokingly said, "Is that 7 o'clock tonight or tomorrow 7 o'clock sometime?"

Geesh.

I told her, "I don't know."

Well, 7 o'clock that night passed by. So did 7 o'clock the next morning. So did 7 o'clock that night. She wasn't happy. Neither was I.

I told the Lord, "This isn't funny." "When can we get the power and lights back on?"

Nada.

So, it went on for the third day. Then the fourth. It was getting less "funny" all the time.

Then the fifth. Then the sixth. Then sometime on the seventh day, the power came back on.

Oh Lord, "You're so 'funny'."

NOT.

I hope you're getting the point.

We *ONLY* see in a Mirror dimly.

We *ONLY* hear in part.

We *ONLY* see in part.

We *ONLY* know in part.

We *MUST* always keep that in our minds.

Hence, humility.

GRAYSON THE CAT

Just the other day, on a Saturday morning, my friend, Jack, a good Christian, texted me that Grayson, the cat they were pet sitting for a friend, ran out the door when he let their dogs out at 6 am.

He and his wife looked everywhere in the yard and all around the neighborhood—but could not find Grayson.

Jack asked me to not only pray for Grayson but also for his wife, who was devastated. I told him I would and that I'd ask the Lord to have His angels be on the lookout for and help return Grayson. He appreciated hearing that.

As I prayed, on and off, throughout the day, I got a strong feeling the angels would return Grayson to them at 9 pm that night, in person.

I did NOT tell Jack that.

Because, while the Lord has given me some feelings over the years that came to pass, others did not.

I've made plenty of mistakes. Hopefully, you should've figured that out by now.

As I keep reminding you: I know I'm repeating the same thing, over and over, but you really need to get this firmly and deeply engrained into your mind. We *ONLY* see in a Mirror dimly. We *ONLY* hear in part. We *ONLY* see in part. We *ONLY* know in part.

So, NO ONE ever gets it right all the time. NO ONE.

And, anyone who says otherwise is drunk on their own "Ego Juice".

Jack and family kept looking everywhere throughout the day with no success.

Funny thing.

At 9:23 pm Saturday night, Jack texted me that his twenty-year-old daughter told them she was just sitting in her room and "out of nowhere" Grayson just appeared in the room—just after 9 pm.

Coincidence or a miracle?

How did the cat get back into their house or even find the right house (being a stranger's house in a strange neighborhood) with no one knowing it?

Why 9 pm?

Maybe just another angel doing the Father's bidding, caring for God's children and even their animals.

Are you catching on to the value of humility wrapped around, "I sense", "I feel", and "I believe", versus, "Thus says the Lord"?

BALAAM'S DONKEY

In Numbers 22:20-35, we learn about the prophet Balaam and his donkey,

"God came to Balaam at night and said to him, 'If the men have come to call you, rise up and go with them; but only the word which I speak to you shall you do.'

So Balaam arose in the morning and saddled his donkey and went with the leaders of Moab.

But God was angry because he was going, and the angel of the Lord took his stand in the way as an adversary against him. Now he was riding on his donkey and his two servants were with him.

When the donkey saw the angel of the Lord standing in the way with his drawn sword in his hand, the donkey turned off from the way and went into the field; but Balaam struck the donkey to turn her back into the way.

Then the angel of the Lord stood in a narrow path of the vineyards, with a wall on this side and a wall on that side.

When the donkey saw the angel of the Lord, she pressed herself to the wall and pressed Balaam's foot against the wall, so he struck her again.

The angel of the Lord went further and stood in a narrow place where there was no way to turn to the right hand or the left.

When the donkey saw the angel of the Lord, she lay down under Balaam; so Balaam was angry and struck the donkey with his stick.

And the **LORD** opened the **mouth** of the **donkey**, and she said to Balaam, 'What have I done to you, that you have struck me these three times?'

Then Balaam said to the donkey, 'Because you have made a mockery of me! If there had been a sword in my hand, I would have killed you by now.'

The donkey said to Balaam, 'Am I not your donkey on which you have ridden all your life to this day? Have I ever been accustomed to do so to you?' And he said, 'No.'

Then the **LORD opened** the **eyes** of **Balaam**, and he saw the angel of the Lord standing in the way with his drawn sword in his hand; and he bowed all the way to the ground.

The angel of the Lord said to him, 'Why have you struck your donkey these three times? Behold, I have come out as an adversary, because your way was contrary to me.

But the donkey saw me and turned aside from me these three times. If she had not **turned aside** from me, I would surely have **killed you** just now, and let her live.'

Balaam said to the angel of the Lord, 'I have sinned, for I did not know that you were standing in the way against me. Now then, if it is displeasing to you, I will turn back.'

But the angel of the Lord said to Balaam, 'Go with the men, but you shall speak only the word which I tell you.' So Balaam went along with the leaders of Balak."

In short, Balaam was being offered to be "honored richly" to go to Balak to curse Israel. At first, Balaam sounded so convincing to God that he'd *NEVER* do that to Israel. But as he went with them, *God knew his heart—God knew differently*. And sent an angel with a drawn sword to stop him—to kill him.

Balaam's faithful donkey stopped him three times, before God allowed his donkey to speak to him, looking towards the angel standing in front of

Balaam, ready to kill him.

His faithful donkey saved his life.

So Why Did I Tell You All This About Balaam?

Back in the early Charismatic days, after enjoying the Power and Presence of God in our gatherings, we'd spend a lot of time afterwards just talking and fellowshipping. Not in any rush to go home. No matter how late it was. And it could be late, late, late.

There was a time one night, right after one of these meetings, when I met a well-dressed, visiting older sister. You could tell that she was a very mature, intelligent, and good Believer; whom I'd never met before. This wasn't unusual as many, many new people would come to visit our church from far and wide, as it was the hub in central Ohio where the Lord was moving mightily.

As this sister and I were just fellowshipping, in light conversation, about all that had just happened that night—suddenly—*I felt* the Lord showed me something very serious **I believed** He wanted me to tell her. I considered this before the Lord, in the back of my mind, as we continued to talk. I became convinced that He wanted me to share it.

It was a difficult subject where He wanted me to talk about some very negative spiritual things going on with her. I hesitated, but I had His Peace that passed understanding, confirming to do it.

Slowly, carefully, I addressed the subject.

I did *NOT* say, "Thus says the Lord", even though I felt that sure.

I said, "I believe that the Lord just showed me, *'this and that, and, so and so'.*" Obviously, I will not reveal her problems, secrets, or other concerns here in this book or anywhere, as the Lord doesn't like nor condone gossip.

She looked stunned.

She retreated backwards, as if an arrow had just pierced her heart as she grabbed at her chest.

She looked to regain her composure, not knowing how to deal with the truth just presented her.

Then, it appeared as if a light bulb had switched on.

She ever so slightly, devilishly grinned, as she responded, "I could've, or maybe would've, received what you were saying, if you were a recognized apostle or a recognized prophet. But since you aren't, I just can't receive it."

Relief washed over her face, as if the matter was settled and nothing more could be said.

In that instant, the Lord gave me an answer for her.

I asked her, "Do you remember Balaam's donkey, who talked to him as he was about to be killed by the angel of the Lord sent to stop him?"

She answered, "Yes."

"Well then, just consider me *'an ass'.*"

Now she looked even more stunned than the first time.

I just walked away.

God didn't need me to pronounce "The says the Lord" to provide "special effects." The power of God's [current living] Word is *ALWAYS* more than enough by itself.

I love Papa's humor!

He cracks me up!

[AT BEST] WE SEE THROUGH A MIRROR DIMLY

I mentioned earlier that I'd expand on this subject. So here we go.

WE ONLY SEE IN PART AND KNOW IN PART

Let's revisit First Corinthians 13:12, from earlier, where we read:

"For *NOW* we ***see*** in a ***mirror dimly***, but then face to face; now I ***know*** in ***part***, but then I will ***know*** fully just as I also have been fully ***known***."

As mentioned previously, this verse is far too important to gloss over. Many want to think and say that they *"hear from God"*, as if they have the direct line to Him, and can hear, see, and know *SO MUCH MORE, SO MUCH BETTER, SO MUCH CLEARER* than the rest of all us "common folks."

Again, can't we ALL can hear from God?

YES.

But how well can *ANYONE* see, hear, and know Him? We just learned a lot, but,

Let's dig deeper.

The word ***now*** in the Greek is 'arti' (AR-tee) which means *"Now," "at this moment," "just now."*

The word ***see*** in the Greek is 'blepō' (blep'-ō) which means *"to look [at]," "consider," "facing," "keep on seeing," "looking," "partial," "take care," "take heed," and "watch."*

The word ***mirror*** in the Greek is 'esoptron' (eh'-sop-tron) which means *"a mirror" and "an object for looking into"* which is from the root words 'eis' (ice) which means *"to or into [indicating the point reached* or entered, of place, time, purpose, or result]," "beyond," "continually," "forever," "perpetually," "throughout," and "view"; and 'horaō' (ho-rah'-ō) which means "to see," "perceive," "attend to," "appear," "behold," "watch," and "witnessed."

The word *dimly* in the Greek is 'ainigma' (ah'-ee-nig-mah) which is where we get the word "enigma" and, it also means, "to speak in riddles," "a riddle," and "a person, thing, or situation that is mysterious, puzzling, or ambiguous."

As mentioned, the word *know* in the Greek is 'ginōskō' (ghin-oce'-ko) which means "to come to know," "recognize," "perceive," "aware," "comprehend," "felt," "find," "found," "knew," "know," "knowing," "known," "knows," "learn," "learned," "perceived," "perceiving," "realize," "recognize," as well as meaning "virgin," "kept...a virgin."

The same word *know* in the Hebrew is 'yada' (yah-DAH) which means "to know," "becomes known," "knew," "known," "very well know," as well as, meaning to be "intimate," "cohabit," and "had relations."

The word *part* in the Greek is 'meros' (MEH-ros) which means "to receive one's portion," "a part, share, portion," "partial," "a piece," "some degree," and "some points."

Expanding this verse with the Greek [and Hebrew] could easily lead to its interpretation as,

"For *NOW* [in the current] we are *Looking* at, *Considering*, *PARTIALLY SEEING* through a *Mirror*, indicating the *Point Reached* or *Entered*, of a *Place* or *Time* or *Purpose* or *Result* (perpetually) and can *NOW PARTIALLY PERCEIVE* through a *DIMLY* (blurred) *REFLECTION* of *REALITY* as in a *Riddle* or *Enigma* that will remain *Mysterious*, *Puzzling*, and *Ambiguous*, but then face to face; *NOW* I've come to *Know, Recognize, Comprehend, Perceive* in *Part* (imperfectly), *Receiving* a *Portion*, a *Piece*, and to *Some* (small) *Degree* the *Intimate Relationship* [with God], but then I will *know* fully just as I also have been fully *known*."

Did you get the FULL impact here?

So, to repeat again and again, to the many who say that they *"hear from God"*, have a direct line to Him, and can hear, see, and know *SO MUCH MORE, SO MUCH BETTER,* and *SO MUCH CLEARER* than the rest of us; or even allude to such in the least; are *"HIGH"* or *"DRUNK"*, sucking on their own *"EGO JUICE"*; poured out by the *god* of this world.

This is the time to understand that we must *ABIDE* in genuine humility before God (again covered in the first book in great detail). Unless you humble yourself before God, recognize you are weak, without power in yourself; *ONLY* able to hear, see, and know in part *[AT BEST—EVEN ON OUR VERY BEST DAYS]*, as just described; then you will fall; and you will fail.

LET THE PEACE OF GOD RULE

I've mentioned this multiple times in this and the first book, but the vast importance of this subject necessitates reiteration.

We need to let the Peace of God rule in our hearts and our minds—in all we do; to end captivity; and walk with Papa God.

THE PEACE OF GOD

Expanding from earlier, in Philippians 4:6-7 we're told,

"Do not be anxious about anything, but in every situation, by prayer and petition, with thanksgiving, present your requests to God. And **THE PEACE** of *God*, which transcends **ALL Understanding**, will **Guard** your **Hearts** and your **Minds** in **Christ** *[the **Anointing**]* Jesus."

We need to learn to operate in and live by **THE PEACE** that passes understanding.

We can clearly know what is from God because of **HIS PEACE**—not "a peace."

When we stop and yield our hearts to the Father, He will give us His Peace in the best and worst of times.

So when words, commands, decrees, teachings, or thoughts come from *false Belief Systems, false anointings, false leaders,* or even good brethren who've become *Stockholm-inducted-devotees;* how do we distinguish what's the Truth versus the enemy's indoctrinations via their rulers, demons-in-nations?

*Simply, by **HIS PEACE** that **PASSES UNDERSTANDING.***

This is how we can differentiate God's Truth from the enemy's lies.

As stated previously, we can learn how to tell them apart by knowing God's Word, then sensing if God's Peace that passes understanding is there or not. Remembering the enemy knows God's Word better than us, so the Word by itself is not enough.

WARNING ABOUT "A PEACE"

"A peace" is NOT "THE PEACE."

"THE PEACE" is God's Peace that passes understanding.

Growing up in the church, many would say, "I was praying, and I got a peace." Not good enough. Read a lot more about the failing of "a peace" in the first book.

ALWAYS LISTEN TO THE "OFF" FEELINGS

As discussed, the *"OFF"* feelings or the *"CHECK in your spirit"* are **EXTREMELY IMPORTANT**. Pay attention and listen. Listen closely. This is the Spirit of God inside telling you *"STOP"*, look around, and ask Me if I'm in these things. Then wait for My Peace. If you don't get *The*

Peace—not a peace; then leave. Don't look back.

It's better to choose to go into the wilderness. Let God purge you of the *false Belief Systems.* Than to stay and die [spiritually].

GUARD YOUR HEART

Remember,

*"**THE PEACE** of God, which transcends ALL Understanding, will **GUARD** your hearts and your minds in Christ Jesus."*

Let it.

Listen correctly.

Don't pretend.

Don't be "spiritual".

Don't be "religious".

Walk in the Spirit.

Or don't claim otherwise.

It's time to grow up.

In Proverbs 4:20-23 it says,

"My son, pay attention to what I say; turn your ear to my words.

Do not let them out of your sight, keep them within your heart;

For they are life to those who find them and health to one's whole body.

Above all else, **GUARD** your **Heart** for **EVERYTHING** you do flows from it."

THIS IS THE WORK OF GOD

As mentioned previously, there's a complete chapter in the first book called "REAL FAITH, TRUE FAITH". In there, we go into great detail about what's the genuine faith to be in the Presence and walk with the Father, the True and Living God.

But I will repeat a part of it here.

THE WORK OF GOD

In John 6:28-29 we're told,

"Therefore they said to Him, 'What shall we do, so that we may work the works of God?' Jesus answered and said to them, 'This is the *Work* of *God*, that you *BELIEVE* in Him whom He has sent.'"

Dual Meanings ~ It Works Both Ways

First, it's the *Work* of *God* to reach out to us and it's *ONLY* by the *Work* of *God* that we *BELIEVE*.

Second, for us, the *ONLY Work* of *God* we can do is to *BELIEVE*.

The first is more obvious, the second might not be.

So What Does That Mean?

If God didn't reach out to help us *BELIEVE*—we would *NOT*. We'd wander around this world doing our own thing—none the wiser. His Work of reaching out by Jesus coming and dying for us was going the ultimate distance. Then His continued Work by the Holy Spirit reaching out to us repeatedly is the utmost dedication and commitment for us to come to Him. This is the more obvious one.

The not so obvious one is that the **ONLY** *Work* of *God* we can do is to **BELIEVE**.

You say that makes little sense.

We can do all kinds of things to Work the Works for God.

We can study, pray, attend church, give tithes and offerings, preach the gospel, evangelize, teach, pastor, care for the flock, minister to one another, exercise all the gifts God gives us, and disciple others; as well as, take care of our families, work our jobs as unto Him, etc., etc., etc.

Right?

Wrong!

The people did ask Jesus, "What shall we do, so that we may work the works of God?" But Jesus did not answer that question. He did not tell them about all the "works" plural that they could or should do. Instead, His answer was *"This is THE WORK of God."* **THE WORK** is singular.

As Jesus said, **THE WORK** is to **BELIEVE**. If we don't get this down, then the rest of the "works" are just a total waste of time and energy. They won't impress the Father no matter what you do.

THE HOLY SPIRIT IS OUR HELPER

In John 15:26, Jesus said,

"But when the Comforter (Counselor, **Helper**, Advocate, Intercessor, Strengthener, Standby) comes, Whom I will send to you from the Father, the *Spirit* of *Truth* who comes (proceeds) from the Father, He [Himself] will testify regarding Me."

The Holy Spirit is our Helper. Jesus sent Him to us when he died, resurrected, and ascended to Heaven.

We are to receive Him.

We are to depend upon Him.

We are to cast our cares on Him.

We are to take every thought captive into the obedience [yielding] to Him.

In John 7:38-39 it says,

"He who *BELIEVES* in Me, as the Scripture said, 'From his innermost being will flow rivers of living water.' But this He spoke of the Spirit."

JESUS ONLY DID THE WILL OF THE FATHER

Again, as stated in Matthew 7, Jesus told us,

"Not everyone who says to Me, 'Lord, Lord,' will enter the Kingdom of Heaven, but he who does the will of My Father who is in Heaven will enter.

Many will say to Me on that day, 'Lord, Lord, did we not prophesy, in your name,

And, in your name, cast out demons, and, in your name, perform many miracles?'

And then, I will declare to them, 'I never *KNEW* you; depart from me, you who practice lawlessness.'"

The word *KNEW* is the same word for *KNOW* in the Greek 'ginōskō' (ghin-oce-ko), meaning *"to come to know," "recognize," "perceive," "aware," "comprehend," "felt," "find," "found," "knew," "know," "knowing," "known," "knows," "learn," "learned," "perceived," "perceiving," "realize," "recognize,"* as well as meaning *"virgin," "kept...a virgin."*

In John 14:31 it says,

"But I do as the Father has commanded Me, so that the world may know (be convinced) that I love the Father and that I do only what the Father has instructed Me to do. [I act in full agreement with His orders.]"

In John 5:19 it says,

"Therefore Jesus answered and was saying to them, 'Truly, truly, I say to you, the Son can do nothing of Himself, unless it is something He sees the Father doing; for whatever the Father does, these things the Son also does in like manner.'"

In John 5:30 it says,

"I can do nothing on My own initiative. As I hear, I judge; and My judgment is just, because I do not seek My own will, but the will of Him who sent Me."

In John 8:29 it says,

"And He who sent Me is with Me; He has not left Me alone, for I always do the things that are pleasing to Him."

In John 8:55 it says,

"And you have not come to know Him, but I **KNOW** Him and keep His word."

This word **KNOW** in the Greek is 'oida' (oh-da), and is like 'ginōskō' (ghin-oce-ko) above, meaning *"to have seen or perceived, hence to know," "become learned," "knew," "knowing," "understand."*

Meaning it's out of this deep intimate relationship with the Father that Jesus **KNEW** Him and therefore **ONLY** functioned out of that **BELIEF**. That intimate relationship—that issues Real True Faith. Seeing and doing **ONLY** what the Father was doing.

WHAT IS THE WILL OF THE FATHER?

In John 6:38, 40 it says,

"For I have come down from heaven, not to do My own will, but the will of Him who sent Me.

For this is the will of My Father, that everyone who beholds the Son and *BELIEVES* in Him will have eternal life."

In John 14:11-14 it says,

"*BELIEVE* Me that I am in the Father and the Father is in Me; otherwise *BELIEVE* because of the works themselves.

Truly, truly, I say to you, he who *BELIEVES* in Me, the works that I do, he will do also; and greater works than these he will do; because I go to the Father.

Whatever you ask in My name, that will I do, so that the Father may be glorified in the Son. If you ask Me anything in My name, I will do it."

Be sure to read the first book to see the rest of this information so you can get the full impact of these truths for your life.

LET'S TALK "PERFECTION" AGAIN

It's now time, as promised, to link this back to the earlier chapter.

This is where we can combine what we've just (re) learned to "THE 'WORK' NEEDS TO BE PERFECT" in the chapter, "IT'S NOT BASED ON PERFECTION".

Since we see what the *WORK* is, which is to *BELIEVE*, we can now begin to realize how that relates to *"Perfection."*

The *WORK* to *BELIEVE* only comes from God; and that only comes after our *CHOICE* and *YIELDING* to Him—which even He initiates. The convergence of these elements gives us the opportunity to have that deep intimate relationship of *KNOWING* and *WALKING* with the Father. Therefore, in each of those moments, when we get out of the way and experience deep intimacy with Him is where we find *Perfection*.

Therefore, the *WORK* needs to be *"Perfect"*—the *Works* do *NOT!*

Which is *NOW* possible—*ONLY* because the *Holy Spirit* is helping us to *BELIEVE, CHOOSE*, and *YIELD* in this moment.

LIVE FOR, IN, AND OUT OF THE PRESENCE OF GOD

WARNING

You need to know that you will come and go from one bondage to another as the pendulum swings unless you keep your eyes fixed on the Lord.

Then, and only then, can the Holy Spirit *GUIDE* you through all the pitfalls that await you.

Yet exactly like the *WORK* of God, both can *ONLY* happen through the *Helper* [the Holy Spirit] by taking every thought *Captive* when yielding to Him.

I AM AND WE ARE

Another upcoming book, *BREATHE THE SPIRIT*, will cover this in depth.

In short, for this book, we need to understand that God's name is *"I AM."*

In Exodus 3:13-14,

"Then Moses said to God, 'Behold, I am going to the sons of Israel, and I will say to them, "The God of your fathers has sent me to you." Now they may say to me, "What is His name?" What shall I say to them?'

God said to Moses, *'I AM WHO I AM';* and He said, 'Thus you shall say to the sons of Israel, *"I AM* has sent me to you."'"

God is I AM.

Meaning He's *ALWAYS* existed and will *ALWAYS* exist.

He just IS.

God doesn't need to do something special to be who He is, **He just IS.** He's always in the Presence of the Son, the Holy Spirit, and Himself. Which should be obvious.

So, when God calls us to be in His Presence, He just wants us to be *"WE ARE."*

Yes, we're to seek after Him. We're to thirst after Him. We're to yield to come into His Presence. But when we get there, He doesn't want us to do "something" or "anything."

*He just wants us "**TO BE**" as **HE IS**.*

Just there.

Nothing else.

Enjoying Him and His Presence and the Son and the Spirit.

To Be, or Not To Be

"To be, or not to be, that is the question" as Shakespeare wrote in Hamlet. While an excellent play, these words should standalone and ring throughout our beings every day. *To be* in the *Presence* of the *Father*, the *Son* and the *Spirit*, or *not to be*. As always, it's a matter of *CHOICE* and *YIELDING*.

IF YOU HAVE EYES TO SEE, AND EARS TO HEAR

He wants us to be in the place that

WE ARE with I AM.

CHAPTER
TWENTY-ONE

IT'S NOT UP TO US

I F IT WAS,

WE COULD NEVER DO IT

WHAT "WE DESERVE"

In the first book, we saw a chapter titled, "NEVER BASED ON WHAT 'WE DESERVE'". I'll repeat some of it here.

We Deserve Nothing

As stated previously, we cannot do anything to be worthy enough or good enough to reach God, let alone stay in His Presence.

"For by Grace you have been saved through faith; and that not of yourselves, it is the *GIFT* of *GOD; NOT* as a *RESULT* of [any] *WORKS*, so that no one may boast."

And,

"All OUR RIGHTEOUSNESS [our best deeds of rightness and justice] are like *FILTHY RAGS* or a polluted garment."

Unworthy Servants

As stated in Luke 17, you need to wrap your head around this—we will *ALWAYS* be unworthy servants—*NO MATTER WHAT.*

"When *YOU* have done *EVERYTHING* that was assigned and commanded you, say, we are *UNWORTHY SERVANTS* [possessing no merit, for we have not gone beyond our obligation]; We have [merely] *DONE* what was *OUR DUTY* to do."

It Was, Is, and Never Will Be Based on Us

Not "how good."

Not "how religious."

Or even, "how yielded."

We were.

Are.

Or ever will be.

THE LAW OF THE SPIRIT

The law of the Spirit of life in Christ has set you free.

Romans 8:1-17 says,

"Therefore there is now no condemnation for those who are in **Christ** *[the* **Anointing***]* Jesus.

For the law of the *Spirit* of life in *Christ [the Anointing]* Jesus has set you free from the law of sin and of death.

For what the Law could not do, weak as it was through the flesh, God did: sending His own Son in the likeness of sinful flesh and as an offering for sin, He condemned sin in the flesh,

So that the *requirement* of the *Law* might be *fulfilled* in us, who do not *Walk* according to the flesh but *according* to the *Spirit*.

For those who are according to the flesh set their minds on the things of the flesh, but those who are according to the Spirit, the things of the Spirit.

For the mind set on the flesh is death, but the *Mind set* on the *Spirit* is *Life* and *Peace*,

Because the mind set on the flesh is hostile toward God; for it does not subject itself to the law of God, for it is not even able to do so,

And those who are in the flesh cannot please God.

However, you are not in the flesh but in the Spirit, if indeed the Spirit of God dwells in you. But if anyone does not have the *Spirit* of *Christ (the Anointing)*, he does not belong to Him.

If *Christ (the Anointing)* is in you, though the body is dead because of sin, yet the *spirit* is *alive* because of *righteousness*.

But if the *Spirit* of *Him* who raised Jesus from the dead *dwells* in you, He who raised *Christ (the Anointing)* Jesus from the dead will also give *life* to your *mortal bodies* through *His Spirit* who dwells in you.

So then, brethren, we are under obligation, not to the flesh, to live according to the flesh

For if you are living according to the flesh, you must die; but if by the *Spirit* you are putting to death the deeds of the body, you will live.

For *ALL* who are being *led* by the *Spirit* of *God*, these are sons of God.

For you have not received a spirit of slavery leading to fear again, but you have **received** a **spirit** of **adoption** as **sons** by which we cry out, **"ABBA! FATHER!" ["PAPA!"]**

The **Spirit Himself** testifies with our **spirit** that we are children of God,

And if children, heirs also, heirs of God and fellow heirs with **Christ** *(the Anointing)*, if indeed we suffer with Him so that we may also be glorified with Him."

IT ALL COMES BACK TO CHRIST [AGAIN]

As we've learned repeatedly from the first book through this one, living *IN Christ* (*IN the Anointing*) is the *KEY*.

NOTHING ELSE.

We must learn how to yield—get out of the way—to allow the Spirit of God to flow from our innermost beings. Then and only then can we be in the Presence of the Father and learn to live out of that Presence.

NO ONE ELSE

If we, in the natural, can't do it by ourselves, then

neither can anyone

nor any leader

nor anything

nor any Belief System

do it for us.

THE YIELDED HEART

ONLY THOSE WHO TRULY SEEK HIM WILL FIND HIM

It's not a matter of striving in the flesh, but in seeking by Yielding. And then we will find Him when we are raised up with **Christ *(the Anointing)*.**

"Therefore if you have been raised up with **Christ *(the Anointing)*,** keep seeking the things above, where **Christ *(the Anointing)*** is, seated at the right hand of God.

SET your ***MIND*** on the ***THINGS ABOVE***, not on the things that are on earth.

For you have ***died*** and your ***life*** is ***hidden*** with **Christ *(the Anointing)*** in God.

When **Christ *(the Anointing)*,** who is our life, is ***revealed***, then you also will be ***revealed*** with Him in glory." (Colossians 3:1-4)

ONLY THOSE WHO ARE TRANSFORMED WILL FIND HIM

Be transformed by the renewing of your mind.

"Do not conform to the pattern of this world, but be ***transformed*** by the ***renewing*** of ***your mind***. Then you will be able to ***test*** and ***approve*** what God's will is—his good, pleasing and perfect will." (Romans 12:2 NIV)

In the AMP version, it reads,

"Do not be ***conformed*** to this ***world*** (this age), [fashioned after and adapted to its external, superficial customs], but be ***transformed*** (changed) by the [entire] ***renewal*** of ***your mind*** [by its new ideals and its new attitude], so that you may *prove* [for yourselves] what is the **good** and **acceptable** and **perfect will** of **God**, even the thing which is **good** and **acceptable** and **perfect** [in His sight for you]."

"IT'S WHO YOU YIELD TO"

I know you maybe tired of me repeating this. But it's imperative to your spiritual health that you remember everything the first book taught you about **Yielding**.

Please go back and review. Read the full chapter, "IT'S A MATTER OF CHOICE AND YIELDING" which will teach you all you need to know. Where you'll see, again, that **Choice** and **Yielding** are the **ONLY** powers we have in the spiritual realm.

> That "**Choice** and **Yielding** are a Truism in Everything."

And the truth taught about the "Two Golden Pipes", from Zechariah 4; where we saw we are nothing more than "**Golden Pipes** (**Vessels**, **Conduits**, or **Channels**), which empty the **Golden Oil** from themselves."

You must learn the secret repeatedly taught from the manual:

"We're a vessel to whomever we yield."

Again, as Jesus told us, we're a vessel to one source or the other.

"*WHOEVER* is *NOT WITH ME* is *AGAINST ME*, and whoever does not gather with me scatters."

Therefore, there's no middle ground. As I mentioned earlier, you can't have it your own way—this isn't Burger King®.

The enemy is desperately working overtime to obtain direct control over you by getting you to **Yield** to the wrong spiritual things—even in the churches; by adding just a little misdirection; by religion or religiosities; by "great spiritual" distractions; by denominations; by any offshoots; by any tangents, etc.; no matter here, there, and everywhere.

The enemy doesn't care what we do just as long as none of us stop, repent, and ask the Lord to come into and live throughout our daily lives with Him—by His Spirit. Giving over control, *Yielding* to Him, allowing Him to clean up our lives and get rid of the oppressing, possessing, and *false Belief Systems* that the enemy would like us to remain under.

Conversely, if we consistently *Yield* ourselves to *Christ (the Anointing)* and *allow* the *Holy Spirit* to *flow* through us, filling and changing these areas so that *rivers* of *living water flow* from our *innermost being*, we will have the *Full Life* in *Christ (the Anointing)* promised to us.

Noting again *Yielding* is an ongoing, lifelong, daily, moment-by-moment process which leads to *Sanctification*. And we will *NEVER* complete that process while we live on Earth.

So, let's garner this same mind—it's about *Seeking*, *Yielding*, *Believing*, and *Walking* with the Lord [or allowing Him to walk with us] throughout this life. Let us learn to focus on Him versus all else.

Remember: Since you can never be good enough on your own—stop trying—start *Yielding*.

LET THE WATERS FLOW

RIVERS OF LIVING WATERS

We've discussed this many times to this point in this book and the first, so we won't spend a lot of time here. This is just a reminder that we *MUST* have the *Holy Spirit flowing* from our *spirit*—where we were sealed; through our soul, heart, mind, thoughts, and feelings; to, and through, our body; and beyond.

To overflow, as Jesus said, and I repeat, from John 7, where,

"Jesus stood and cried out, saying, 'He who **BELIEVES** in Me, as the Scripture said, from his innermost being will flow **Rivers** of **Living Water.**' But this He spoke of the **SPIRIT** *[the ANOINTING],* whom those who believed in Him were to receive."

Once again, this is *ALL* about *Choice* and *Yielding*. You cannot make the Spirit of God flow through you. And no matter how much He wants to flow through you, He cannot and will not do so unless you *choose* to *get out* of the *way*.

"RELAX"

CHOOSE, YIELD AND THEN RELAX IN GOD'S PRESENCE

Now it's time to *Relax*.

Since it was NEVER up to us.

NEVER able to be created by us.

NEVER able to be achieved by us.

NEVER able to be obtained by us.

NEVER able to be procured by us.

NEVER able to be acquired by us.

Then *Relax*.

Relax in the Presence of the Father.

Let Him do the WORK in you!

CHAPTER TWENTY-TWO

THERE WILL BE JOY IN THE MORNING!

After the Wilderness.

After the Mourning.

There will be Joy in the Morning!

"I WILL EXTOL YOU, O Lord, for You have lifted me up and have not let my foes rejoice over me.

O Lord my God, I cried to You and You have healed me.

O Lord, You have brought my life up from Sheol (the place of the dead);

You have kept me alive, that I should not go down to the pit (the grave).

Sing to the Lord, O you saints of His, and give thanks at the remembrance of His holy name.

For **His anger** is but for a **moment**, but **His Favor** is for a **Lifetime** [and in **His Favor** is **Life**]. Weeping may endure for a night, but **JOY COMES** in the **MORNING**.

As for me, in my prosperity [in my own ego and pride] I said, I shall never be moved.

But by Your favor, O Lord, You have established me as a strong mountain;

You hid Your face, and I was troubled.

I cried to You, O Lord, and to the Lord I made supplication.

What profit is there in my blood, when I go down to the pit (the grave)?

Will the dust **praise You**?

Will it declare **Your truth** and **faithfulness** to men?

Hear, O Lord, have **mercy** and be **gracious** to me! O Lord, be my **Helper**!

You have turned my **MOURNING** into **dancing** for me;

You have put off my sackcloth and **girded me** with **gladness**,

To the end that my **tongue** and my **heart** and everything glorious within me may **sing praise** to **You** and **not** be **silent**.

O Lord my God, I will give **thanks** to **You forever**." (Psalms 30:1-12)

And in Second Corinthians 4:14-18,

"[Be] assured that He who raised up the Lord Jesus will raise us up also with Jesus and bring us [along] with you into **His Presence**.

For all [these] things are [taking place] for your sake, so that the more Grace (divine favor and spiritual blessing) extends to more and more people and multiplies through the many, that more thanksgiving may increase [and redound] to the glory of God.

Therefore, we do not become **Discouraged** (utterly **Spiritless**, **Exhausted**, and **Wearied** out through **Fear**). Though our outer man is [progressively] decaying and wasting away, yet our **Inner Self** is **Being** [progressively] **Renewed Day** after **Day**.

For our **light, momentary affliction** (this slight distress of the passing hour) is Ever More and More **Abundantly Preparing** and **Producing** and **Achieving** for Us an **Everlasting Weight** of **Glory** [Beyond **ALL Measure**, Excessively Surpassing **ALL Comparisons** and **ALL Calculations**, a Vast and Transcendent **Glory** and **Blessedness** Never to **Cease!**],

Since we **Consider** and **Look** not to the Things that are Seen but to the **Things** that are **Unseen**; for the things that are visible are temporal (brief and fleeting), but the **Things** that are **Invisible** are **Deathless** and **Everlasting**."

~~~~~

As a [literal] forty-year survivor of the wilderness, I can attest while it can be extremely hard and its purpose is to break *ALL* of your pride, ego, and false beliefs; I highly recommend you...

EMBRACE THE WILDERNESS.

THE WILDERNESS AND THE PROCESS WILL BE WORTH IT!

CHOOSE TO LET GOD DO IT IN YOU.

IF YOU HAVE EARS TO HEAR, JOY COMES THROUGH THE MOURNING.

IF YOU HAVE EYES TO SEE, THE JOURNEY IS THE DESTINATION.

AND IN THE END, YOU WILL HAVE JOY IN THE MORNING!

These are not just empty platitudes, they are the results from allowing the Spirit of God to do this *FULL* work in you.

FINAL NOTE #1

Many readers likely hoped this book offered a rapid "microwave" solution to achieving lasting freedom from captivity. Probably so they could dismiss this matter and move on to God's "next great teachings," "areas of learning," "important new subjects," "new secrets," "mysteries," "revelations," "ministries," "gifts," or "more important things."

But, unfortunately, it didn't and it won't.

You must understand, **choosing** to **go through** the **wilderness** to **gain freedom** from **captivity** is a "slow-cooker", "crock pot" process. And, when you have eyes to see, embracing the wilderness is more than a process—it's the procurement of the goal.

THEREFORE EMBRACE THE WILDERNESS

The wilderness is the vehicle to get you to the goal; which is getting and maintaining an intimate relationship with *PAPA*. Because amid the wilderness, you'll discover the deep, intimate relationship your spirit has yearned for with **PAPA** accomplished by the **WORK** of His Spirit in you. Only there will you find *ALL* the answers to *ALL* the mysteries of life and the universe in **Christ** *(the **Anointing**)*.

And, in case you haven't figured it out by now, walking with PAPA has ALWAYS been the Next Great Thing.

There is Nothing better.

There is NO Greater Secret, Mystery or Revelation to be had.

Therefore, don't look to avoid the wilderness and move on.

YET STILL, THERE MAY BE MORE TO COME

Not that I'm asking to go continuously—I'm not a masochist. But I'm determined that if I need to go into more wildernesses as the years continue, to be rid of more garbage, so that I can be closer to **PAPA**, to increase our intimate relationship, then so be it.

Therefore, my recommendation to you is to quit fighting and embrace the "crock pot".

FINAL NOTE #2

After you find this FREEDOM for yourself,

Share the Good News!

Bring all who you will.

Bring all who are willing.

ABOUT THE AUTHOR

HI, I'M TOM SNOW

FIRST, LET ME INTRODUCE MYSELF

I'm a conservative Believer and not part of any organized religion or denomination. As a Jewish Christian, I believe that there is one God who created all; and all are equal in God's creation. That there is only one True Church which is the Body of Christ ~ of which All True Believers are a part. I believe in God's Light that dispels darkness and binarily separates Truth from lies. I believe we not only have a spiritual responsibility in the Church but also equally in the world.

In fifty-plus years, I've been tested in many ways, gone to hell and back, and lived to talk about it. Walking with the Lord is SIMPLE, it's just not EASY. The road is narrow. The works written and coming result from being humbled and learning over those many years, and still learning today, tomorrow, and until His return. My goal is to share what little I've learned along the way to help equip other Believers to learn to Walk in the Anointing, then Stand in God's Authority.

While many are chasing a million different answers in a million different ways, there's only ONE. ALL the Greatest Mysteries, Wisdom, Understandings, and Secrets of God and the Universe are revealed inside ONE Simple Truth: being IN CHRIST. Hence, I want to live my life in the Presence and the Heart of the Father, Papa God.

SECOND, HERE'S WHAT I'VE DONE

I'm the owner of a software design company—and have been in hardware and software design for over 45 years. I'm an engineer, inventor, entrepreneur, and fisherman; but most importantly, I love the Lord, my beautiful wife, my five children, and my eight grandchildren.

AND NOWADAYS, I'M WRITING BOOKS AS THE LORD DIRECTS.

LEAVE A REVIEW

HOW WOULD YOU REVIEW SET THE CAPTIVES FREE?

"This book will challenge everything you believe about church and freedom."

"This book will cause controversy. Those being set free will love it. Those wanting to maintain captivity will hate it."

How did the book affect you?

Scan to Review SET THE CAPTIVES FREE

Are you being set free or someone wanting to maintain captivity?

Be honest with yourself and review accordingly so others can be Set Free as well.

Thank you for reading & reviewing SET THE CAPTIVES FREE. – Tom

www.ingramcontent.com/pod-product-compliance
Lightning Source LLC
Chambersburg PA
CBHW070548130626
46556CB00001B/68